Hildebrandt International

ANATOMY
OF A LAW FIRM
MERGER

HOW TO MAKE OR BREAK THE DEAL

—————— **Third Edition** ——————

LAW PRACTICE MANAGEMENT SECTION
MARKETING · MANAGEMENT · TECHNOLOGY · FINANCE

Commitment to Quality: The Law Practice Management Section is committed to quality in our publications. Our authors are experienced practitioners in their fields. Prior to publication, the contents of all our books are rigorously reviewed by experts to ensure the highest quality product and presentation. Because we are committed to serving our readers' needs, we welcome your feedback on how we can improve future editions of this book. We invite you to fill out and return the comment card at the back of this book.

Cover design by Andrew Alcala, ABA Publishing.

Library of Congress Cataloging-in-Publication Data
Anatomy of a Law Firm Merger: How to Make or Break the Deal, Third Edition. Hildebrandt International: Library of Congress Cataloging-in-Publication Data is on file.

ISBN 1-59031-377-1

15 14 13 12 11   5 4 3 2

Discounts are available for books ordered in bulk. Special consideration is given to state bars, CLE programs, and other bar-related organizations. Inquire at Book Publishing, American Bar Association, 321 North Clark Street, Chicago, Illinois 60610.

Contents

Chapter 1
Why Law Firms Should Consider Merging   1

Chapter 2
Strategic Merger Assessment   9

Chapter 3
Initiating the Merger 19

Chapter 4
Evaluating the Merger 29

Chapter 5
Historical Financial Analysis   55

Chapter 6
Developing the Pro Forma Projections   71

Chapter 7
The Economic Balance Sheet   81

Chapter 8
Getting to a Decision   89

Chapter 9
Integrating the Firms   97

Chapter 10
Integrating Administration and Technology   117

List of Exhibits

Preface

A well-planned merger can reap many benefits for the merging firms. This book discusses the many legitimate business reasons why firms should consider merger.

In this book a merger is a consolidation or joining together of two practices, regardless of the sizes of the groups merging. If one firm is significantly larger than the other, the transaction is probably an acquisition rather than a merger, although for political reasons, it may be referred to as a merger. The same is true when a small spin-off group joins an existing firm; the transaction is referred to as a merger, although it may be simply an acquisition.

To avoid confusion, we will not distinguish among *merger, acquisition,* and *lateral acquisition*. The principles discussed here apply equally to all cases, although perhaps in varying degrees. In addition, we will use the terms *merger discussions* and *merger negotiations* synonymously. We use the term *partners* rather than *partners/shareholders, partnerships* rather than *partnership/professional corporation* or *association,* and *partnership agreement* rather than *partnership agreement/buy-sell agreement*. The concepts are similar, regardless of whether the firm is practicing as a partnership or a professional corporation.

Our purpose is to provide guidance to firms of all sizes. Naturally, the process is more complex for large firms. The basic process remains the same, however. The major difference is that small firms can usually get through merger discussions and make decisions more quickly than can large firms. As much as possible throughout the text, we comment on significant differences occasioned by firm size.

This book was written to help firms decide whether they should consider merger, why merger might or might not work for them, and how to go about not only making the decision to merge, but also making the many other decisions involved in completing the merger and ultimately integrating the merged firm. It provides information on every aspect of mergers, from why a firm should consider merger, to making the decision to merge, to analyzing whether the merger makes sense, to arriving at the decision, to integrating the two firms. The book discusses what to do and what not to do, step by step.

- ◆ Chapter 1, "Why Law Firms Should Consider Merging," examines the right and wrong reasons to merge.
- ◆ Chapter 2, "Strategic Merger Assessment," discusses the importance for a firm contemplating merger to analyze its strengths and weaknesses, to know itself and its clients, to understand its own culture and the significance of its culture in the context of merger, and to have specific goals for a merger.
- ◆ Chapter 3, "Initiating the Merger," identifies sources of potential merger candidates and evaluating merger prospects, including the advantages and disadvantages of a firm handling its own search or using the services of an outside organization.
- ◆ Chapter 4, "Evaluating the Merger," examines the analysis process, the role of the merger committee, the key issues to be resolved, and the potential deal breakers.
- ◆ Chapter 5, "Historical Financial Analysis," addresses the importance of the historical financial analysis as part of the analysis process and discusses the benchmarks used for this evaluation and how to use them to test financial strength and identify potential problem areas.
- ◆ Chapter 6, "Developing the Pro Forma Projections," explains the importance of making projections and provides a process for developing them.

- ◆ Chapter 7, "The Economic Balance Sheet," explains the concept of an economic balance sheet and how it can be used to assess balance sheet and capital issues between two firms.

- ◆ Chapter 8, "Getting to a Decision," examines the importance of keeping partners informed throughout the merger discussions, since the decision is really a series of decisions made throughout the process. It also discusses the use of a merger notebook to make available to partners in a single packet all information they need to make a decision.

- ◆ Chapter 9, "Integrating the Firms," describes the importance of building a common culture for the new firm and of having an integration plan so that the lawyers in the firm think as members of one firm and practice as a team, sharing clients and practice expertise. The chapter also discusses the significance of a practice management structure designed to promote firm integration.

- ◆ Chapter 10, "Integrating Administration and Technology," deals with combining the administrative functions and technology platforms.

Acknowledgments

Anatomy of a Law Firm Merger was first published in 1992. This Third Edition evidences the ongoing importance of mergers in meeting the strategic goals of law firms of all sizes, both in the United States and in other countries.

This edition of *Anatomy of a Law Firm Merger*, as was the original book, was made possible by the expertise of Hildebrandt International in providing strategic and merger advice to law firms of all sizes in the United States.

The law firm merger expertise of Hildebrandt International is institutional; it cannot be credited to a single person or group of people. That having been said, we acknowledge the time and effort of William G. Johnston and Lisa R. Smith in substantially revising both the Second and Third Editions, and that of Gerry Malone and Howard Mudrick in editing the First Edition.

Why Law Firms Should Consider Merging

Introduction

The legal industry in the United States and globally continues to be in a period of rapid consolidation. More than four times the number of lawyers were practicing in the 250 largest firms in the United States in 2003 than in 1980 (National Law Journal, The NLJ 250). Nearly fifty law firms had 600 or more lawyers in 2003.

As the largest firms continue to grow, the market for legal services is increasingly segmenting. With increased sophistication of clients, increased complexity of legal problems, more public information about the services provided by law firms, and the perceived sophistication of those services, law firms have to compete on a different basis than in the past. Firms are finding that practice depth and breadth, geographic coverage, and other factors are increasingly critical to their success and profitability.

The consolidation we have seen can come from three primary sources. One is lateral movement of lawyers or groups of lawyers from one firm to another. Lawyer mobility accelerated rapidly through the 1990s and into the 2000s and shows no sign of abating. It is driven in part by economic differences among firms but is also driven by partners determining that their practice and clients are better served by a firm that offers a different platform. The second source of consolidation is actually the breakup of weaker firms. As these firms dissolve, their lawyers invariably land at other law firms, thus fueling the growth of those firms. The third source of consolidation—and the topic of this book—is, of course, mergers between two firms. In fact, some firms have done a series of mergers.

The sheer volume of law firm mergers in recent years has been dramatic. There were 71 mergers* in 2000, 82 mergers in 2001, 55 mergers in 2002, and 35 mergers in 2003. While the number has fallen since the peak of 2000 to 2001, the complexity of mergers has increased because the firms involved now are generally larger than firms that merged even five years ago.

The volume of mergers in recent years has created a body of experience and lessons learned in evaluating and completing deals. Because of the time elapsed since many of the mergers, we can evaluate the success of the combinations and develop a set of principles about success factors.

The bottom line is that the most successful mergers are based on clear strategic thinking and create a combined firm that is more competitive along a number of dimensions than either of the legacy firms were. Alternatively, we have seen some mergers succeed when they viewed the combination as a starting point for creating a competitive advantage. The merger itself created the right platform for future growth (or in some cases, elimination of practices that detract from the firm achieving its ultimate vision). It is important to recognize that a merger in and of itself is not a strategy. A merger should only help two firms implement a strategy. To that end, merger is not the right move for all firms.

---

*A merger for this purpose is defined as a combination where the smaller firm had at least five lawyers and one firm was absorbed into the other (as distinct from lateral groups).

It is difficult, if not impossible, to develop a checklist of the right and wrong reasons to merge. Every potential merger and the reasons for it must be analyzed individually. It is possible that a good reason to merge in one situation may be a bad reason to merge in another. However, the firm that contemplates merger without strategic thinking is unlikely to succeed. It is important to be very frank in the merger assessment process and be willing to walk away from a deal that does not make sense for the firm.

An important lesson learned in past discussions is that with strategic vision and a strong business case, the negotiation process generally goes much more smoothly. When both firms are excited about the opportunities that will be created by the combination, the deal points became less important, and both firms are more likely to be flexible in addressing them.

The Right Reasons to Merge

A firm's strategic planning process should focus on identifying the competitive strengths (and weaknesses) of the firm that create opportunities to build a competitive position in the ever-changing marketplace for legal services. Once the firm has identified its desired competitive position, it can determine the implications of that choice. Sometimes, although not always, a merger will emerge as a way to achieve some aspect of a firm's vision. For example, a merger might be a way to:

1. Enhance the firm's competitive position in one or more of its existing markets.
2. Fill gaps in expertise and increase specialization.
3. Add complementary practices or services.
4. Expand geographically, sometimes with the goal of solidifying the firm's position in its home markets.
5. Increase or diversify the client base, attracting clients neither firm would attract on its own.
6. Solidify relationships with clients common to both firms.

7. Enhance the level of sophistication of the work through breadth and depth of services (although this needs to be evaluated quite critically in the merger process).

Increase Expertise and Specialization

Many firms direct their marketing efforts to developing more business from existing clients, either directly or through referrals. Clients demand a broad range of specialized services. To ensure that they can service increased business, firms must analyze their professional resources and match expertise with need. Specialization is increasingly a key to attracting and retaining clients.

One viable strategy in law firms is to focus on providing a wide range of legal services to specific industry groups. This approach allows lawyers in the firm to become extremely knowledgeable about the trends, opportunities, special problems, special needs, and other idiosyncrasies of that industry. The lawyers can become business counselors to their clients. They can help the clients anticipate, and therefore avoid, legal problems. Such a focus often means that a firm must add expertise in a specific area to service clients' needs. For example, if a client anticipates that it will face more environmental issues in the next few years, the firm may need an environmental practice.

The industry focus, and the fact that clients hire individual lawyers with recognized expertise in their fields, has increased the importance of specialization. A firm's planning process often identifies a specific gap in expertise. For example, the firm may identify a need for several experienced litigation lawyers. The easiest way to fill this need may be to find a litigation firm or group. In its planning process, the firm may also identify complementary practices that would allow the firm to diversify but would not change the firm's focus.

Expand Geographic Presence

Law firms typically move into a new geographic area for one of the following reasons:

   ◆ To take advantage of opportunities in major business centers.

- To follow one or more of the firm's large clients.
- To develop a statewide, regional, or national presence.
- To expand representation of large existing clients in other cities.
- To develop a conduit for a current or anticipated international practice.

Geographic expansion has become a way of life for midsize and large law firms. While it is less common for small firms, some smaller firms believe that they must eventually expand geographically to become more competitive and to hold their current client base.

Often, firms that decide to expand geographically find it more effective to expand through merger. It is not unusual for a small firm to be acquired as the base in opening a branch office. The out-of-town firm needs a local presence to help it become established as a competitor. A major advantage of opening a branch through merger is acquiring an existing client base. This approach also provides a cash flow that can be used to help fund the immediate cost of merging, which reduces the need to borrow to provide working capital or fund one-time merger costs.

Regardless of the reason for geographic expansion, however, the decision should not be based on impulse but on business reasons. For example, following a client to another city might make sense, but the client's move should not be the sole reason for the law firm's expansion. The firm must know the client well enough to know its plans and must ensure that the move will further solidify its relationship with the client. Before following a client to another city, firms need to answer the following questions:

- Is keeping the client a good enough reason?
- Will the office provide other opportunities?
- Does the available business fit the firm's goals?
- Does such a move fit the firm's overall strategic plan?

It is particularly important to critically evaluate the opportunities in another city when the city has a smaller business base than the firm's existing set of offices. Some firms have found that when they open in such a market, they invariably end up doing more "local" work, which may not be consistent with the firm's overall practice.

Expand the Client Base

Many small and midsize firms experience a shrinking client base for a number of reasons. A few of the causes are larger companies acquiring small-business clients, clients going out of business, clients becoming unable to afford increased rates needed to support a growing firm, clients outgrowing the firm's set of services, and the competitive nature of legal practice. Many small and midsize firms are now competing with larger firms for clients that, in the past, large firms were happy to leave to smaller firms. For many small and midsize firms, the best way to protect their client base may be merger. The ideal merger candidate in this situation may be a firm that needs additional expertise or depth to service its existing clients. Likewise, many large firms find that they are too reliant on one client or one area of practice. The merged firm's increased expertise and specialization may attract clients that neither firm could have attracted on its own.

Enhance Work Sophistication

Increasingly, general counsel are looking for breadth, depth, and experience when making hiring decisions. This can put small and midsize firms at a disadvantage in competing for the top-end work. Some mergers have been driven by firms striving to preserve their position as a top-tier practice.

The Wrong Reasons to Merge

Although the wrong reason to merge in one situation may be a good reason to merge in another, generally, the following objectives are the wrong reasons to merge:

1. To follow the trend.
2. To correct internal weaknesses.
3. To control expenses or solve economic problems.
4. To deal with underproductive (or problem) partners.

Follow the Trend

Some firms make the mistake of considering merger because other firms are merging. Partners in some of these firms don't take the time to determine what merger can or can't do for them. This approach can lead to failure. "Because everyone else is doing it" may be the worst reason for merging. A merger is most successful when it is accomplished as part of a long-range business plan. In fact, mergers do not make sense for all firms.

Correct Internal Weaknesses

Generally, mergers make more sense and are easier to accomplish for firms that have corrected their internal weaknesses. In some situations, however, merger can be part of the strengthening process and may resolve the following problems:

- ◆ *Gaps in age and experience levels or partner departures.* A firm with an awkward lawyer mix—e.g., top-heavy and bottom-heavy with a gap in the middle—could have trouble retaining clients if the senior partners are unable to turn client management and responsibility over to young partners. Merger may be a practical solution. Of course, adding lateral partners might solve the problem as well.
- ◆ *Lack of rainmakers.* Because some firms historically emphasized providing legal services and not marketing, many firms (especially small and midsize ones) find that when senior rainmakers retire, no one in the firm can replace them.
- ◆ *Lack of leadership.* Gaining leadership is a surprisingly common reason for considering merger. Many small and midsize firms are beginning to realize that without strong leadership, their future viability is in jeopardy. A merger can often provide the leadership.

Control Expenses or Solve Economic Problems

Some firms look at a merger as a way to reduce expenses. Generally we have found that firms do not achieve expense reductions in a merger, particularly during the integration period of the first year or two. There may be a certain amount of "economy of risk"—that is, the ability to take chances where the economic burden can be spread among more people—as the number of partners increases.

A firm will often focus on reducing expenses because it is not profitable enough to keep its partners happy. Few firms solve their profitability problems through expense control. Normally, profitability issues are revenue related. Few firms will be interested in merging with an unprofitable firm. Merger between two unprofitable firms does not create one profitable firm. On the contrary, the combined firm could end up in a weaker financial position than either of the original firms.

Solve Partnership Problems

Merging to deal with underproductive partners is symptomatic of a firm unable or unwilling to address problems. Most firms will expect problem partners to be dealt with outside of merger discussions. The potential merger may give the firm a scapegoat for dealing with the problem, but it certainly does not eliminate the problem. On the contrary, this attitude can breed resentment in the partners of both firms.

Many recently dissolved firms were involved in merger discussion shortly before their demise. The merger discussions were not the cause of the demise; rather, the stronger firm realized that the risks of their merger outweighed the benefits because the weaker firm had too many unresolved issues. Few firms these days want to take on someone else's management burdens.

Conclusion

The most successful mergers are those that have created a firm with a clear competitive position. To accomplish this, the first step is to know what you are trying to achieve, then determine how you will achieve it. This is more difficult than it sounds.

Strategic Merger Assessment | 2

Introduction

As we discussed in Chapter 1, a merger should be the outcome of strategic thinking. Before a firm can determine what type of merger candidate it is looking for, it must first understand its own needs. This point may seem obvious, but many firms assume that they know and understand their needs without taking a fresh look at themselves. The partners must thoroughly examine their firm to assess its strengths, weaknesses, and plans for future success.

As part of the self-examination process, the firm must assess its resources (that is, its people, practice, clients, and opportunities). This assessment serves several functions:

- ◆ It helps develop the business case for a merger.
- ◆ It helps identify the characteristics of the ideal merger firm.

◆ It helps the firm address and correct internal weaknesses before embarking on a merger search.

◆ It helps the firm communicate key strengths to candidate firms.

◆ It helps the partners focus on some difficult internal issues that may be obstacles in any merger negotiation.

◆ It helps the partners learn a great deal about their own firm.

A firm considering merger should analyze a number of areas and have available certain information before it begins planning. Most firms probably do not analyze their practices and lawyers to the extent discussed here, but unless a firm develops a detailed understanding of these areas, it will have difficulty providing the information necessary for merger negotiations.

The Firm's Practice

Analysis of the firm's practice affects all partners, and it is important that they be involved in the process. Two ways to solicit partners' views are with interviews and surveys. Exhibit 1 (page 125) shows the types of questions typically asked in this exercise. (Exhibits are presented in numeric order at the back of this book and are also on the accompanying diskette.) Written responses to a survey, however, may not provide enough useful information. Practice leaders or members of the strategic planning committee should follow up with one-on-one discussions with partners. Small practice group meetings can be helpful in building consensus within the group about strong and weak practice areas, client profitability, and future client needs. Sometimes firms will want to include associates in the process as well.

Client Base

The firm must know its client base. That means identifying major clients by annual volume of business for at least three years, types of work being done for clients, and practice expertise required now and in the future to service the clients. This analysis allows the firm to identify any weaknesses it has in servicing clients, especially gaps in expertise and depth, and to identify opportunities for additional work. This exercise helps the firm focus on the practice expertise it must seek in a merger, a critical component of the merger candidate profile.

Grouping clients by industry may help the firm identify opportunities for targeting potential clients in specific industries. Especially in small and midsize firms, focusing on a market niche can be critical for future success. Expanded service to a specific industry can be accomplished with the right merger.

Some firms are taking the wise step of talking to their clients as part of this process. Firms that have taken this approach have found it tremendously valuable. We have found that there is often a significant gap between the firm's view of itself or its relationship with its key clients and the clients' view of both of these.

Practice Expertise

The firm must also know its practices and the level of expertise and experience in each. This information can be gained by:

- Analyzing the work the firm is currently doing and categorizing it by practice area.
- Categorizing the type of work each lawyer is doing.
- Defining each lawyer's experience.
- Determining the level of each lawyer's competence. For instance, can the lawyer handle only routine matters, or can the lawyer first-chair a matter in this area?

Usually, the practice assessment reveals current practice strengths and weaknesses. When a firm is considering merger as a strategic alternative, the practice assessment may place the firm in a better position to identify appropriate merger candidates. The assessment can also help a firm anticipate future practice needs. For example, a firm with a cadre of clients in an emerging market may identify a lack of expertise in corporate financing transactions. As a result, the firm could target potential merger partners that not only supplement the firm's current practice, but also offer the kind of expertise clients may need in the future—in this case, corporate finance. It is very important that a practice assessment be framed by the practice's competitive position in the market-place. Client interviews can help in this regard, as can an assess-ment of competitors' practices.

The Firm's Economics

A critical component of the strategic assessment process is an analysis of the firm's economic health. A number of key financial in-dicators can be used as a barometer to test economic health, and these are discussed in Chapter 5. Not all law firms are the same, and the application of these benchmarks and appropriateness of these data for each firm may be different. However, analyzing these types of indicators will put the firm in a much better position to make informed decisions. It is important not to look at these indi-cators individually; they should be examined as a whole. Typically this means examining at least three years' historical financial in-formation. One of the most significant benefits of the historical analysis is to identify trends in the firm's performance.

Again, it is important to look at the firm's financial perform-ance in the context of the marketplace. Firms that have had flat or slightly increased financial performance often find that the strong performance of other firms in their market or nationally has cre-ated a significant gap.

The Firm's Culture

Before the practice of law came to be generally viewed as a busi-ness, lawyers didn't pay much attention to firm culture. Lawyers had tremendous autonomy, which they guarded jealously. The founding partners set the tone, and there was usually little incen-tive to change. The dynamics of the current legal industry have changed that, although lawyers are most likely to feel the impact of culture when going from one firm to another or when the culture of their own firm is changing.

The firm's culture determines, among other things, the following:

- Whether the firm is an institution or simply a group of lawyers sharing space.
- The autonomy individual lawyers have and the extent to which they are accountable to other partners for the management of their individual practices.
- The group's work ethic and working environment.
- The extent to which clients belong to the firm or to the individual lawyers.
- The level of restrictions on work intake and acceptance of new clients.
- The partner compensation system.
- The firm's marketing activities.
- The extent to which partners are involved in day-to-day firm operations, including both management and administration.
- Associate training, supervision, and ultimately, admission to partnership.

More than anything, the firm's culture is an attitude—the philosophical approach to the practice and to people. It is the sum of the interrelationships between and among the lawyers, the working environment, firm governance, business management, practice management, profitability, and ultimately, success or failure.

A merger may create cultural change that some partners are unwilling or afraid to accept. It is important that all partners recognize this possibility because merger-related departures of key partners could outweigh the positive effects of any merger. At the same time, there may be partners whose practices don't fit the strategy of the combined firm, and whose departures should be expected. Partners also need to keep in mind that culture is constantly changing and the firm's culture is likely to change whether or not it does a merger.

It is difficult to define a culture, but it is important for the firm to understand how it might or might not fit with another firm.

Other Areas

In addition to knowing its practice strengths and weaknesses and possessing a good understanding of its lawyer resources, the firm must have a good understanding of its internal operations. The firm must be in a position to discuss, in detail, its historical and philosophical approach to each of the following areas:

- ◆ Firm structure and management, decision making, the future roles of leaders, and the future leaders themselves.
- ◆ Partner compensation, capitalization, and all aspects of withdrawal, including death, disability, retirement, and voluntary and involuntary withdrawal.
- ◆ Organization and management of its practice (the delivery of legal services), including client and case acceptance, the use of engagement letters, pricing, billing and collection guidelines, delegation, quality control systems, and general practice supervision.
- ◆ Its associate and paralegal programs, including recruiting, orientation, training, supervision, evaluation, compensation, and promotion.
- ◆ Administrative management, office policies and procedures, the roles of administrative personnel, and the way those roles complement the management of the firm and practice disciplines.

Merger Goals and Objectives

In identifying the goals for the merger and in developing the firm's practice profile and lawyer profiles, the firm may discover internal problems, such as ineffective practice management or an outdated governance structure. These types of problems must be identified before a merger because the resolution of these issues will bring about change in the firm. For example, if the firm changes its governance structure to centralized governance by a small group, the firm's partners must become comfortable with the new management approach. It is better if the firm makes this type of change before it enters into merger discussions, since it may take some time for the partners to become accustomed to the new structure. Another consideration in making changes is that completion of a merger is not a sure thing. The firm should continue to make decisions that are the right decisions for the firm as a going concern.

The Merger Candidate Profile

The final step of the self-assessment is developing a profile of the ideal merger candidate. The ideal merger partner may not exist, so in an assessment of each merger candidate against the ideal candidate profile, flexibility is important.

The merger candidate profile should address the following candidate characteristics:

- ◆ *Practice mix.* The firm should evaluate the various practices that would enhance its existing mix. Is the firm willing to look at candidates with a general practice with emphasis in a particular area, or only boutique firms?
- ◆ *Geographical location.* The firm should identify the city or cities that fit its strategy. The firm should also determine whether it should consider multiple-office firms, and if so, the preferred locations. Some firms find that the best approach to a new city is a "back door" approach, where the merger partner may not be based in the target city but brings a significant office in that city.
- ◆ *Size and leverage.* These parameters should be set according to the firm's practice profile. The firm may want to further define the ideal candidate's partnership structure (two-tier, etc.).

- *Experience levels of lawyers.* The firm should consider the need to fill gaps in particular classes, as well as law school criteria, including schools attended, law review, specialized degrees, bar admissions, and the like.
- *Client base.* The firm must determine whether it prefers the merger candidate's client base to be local, national, or international and industry-specific or varied. It is also important to identify key clients or industries that would present conflicts for the firm.
- *Financial aspects.* The firm should attempt to estimate the financial status of the ideal merger candidate. Figures to consider are revenue and expenses per lawyer, profits per partner, debt load, and average billable hours. While some differences in key financial metrics can be tolerated in a merger, significant differences can be showstoppers.
- *Culture.* Cultural differences are a leading reason why merger discussions are called off. The firm should define the culture it seeks in its ideal merger partner, or at least define the nonnegotiable aspects of its own culture.
- *Practice and management philosophy.* It is important that the ideal merger candidate have a similar philosophy in these areas or be willing to accept a new philosophy. (These concerns are discussed in more detail in Chapter 4.)
- *An entire firm versus a small group from that firm.* The firm should assess whether it has a preference. A small group of lawyers willing to leave their firm (a *spin-off* group) may be preferable in some cases because the firm can target only the lawyers it wants. For example, a firm wanting to build its environmental practice may be interested only in the environmental lawyers in a particular firm, not the entire firm. Client base, practice expertise, and size of the spin-off group should be considered. Cash flow also should be contemplated: the spin-off group is not likely to bring work in progress or accounts receivable that can be turned into cash immediately after the merger.

Summary

For a law firm to determine in a businesslike manner whether merger will be of benefit, the firm must evaluate its strengths and weaknesses; understand its practice, clients, and culture; and establish clearly defined goals it wishes to reach through merger. Going through this process provides the firm with the information it needs to develop a merger candidate profile and ultimately merge with a compatible firm.

Initiating the Merger 3

Identifying Potential Merger Candidates

Once the firm has determined that merger is an appropriate mechanism for achieving long-term goals and has profiled its ideal merger candidate, the next step is to develop a list of potential merger partners.

A firm can use numerous sources to help identify potential candidates, including the following:

- ◆ *Members of the firm.* Because many of the decisions regarding merger are practice driven, it makes sense for partners in the firm to identify firms they know might fit the firm's merger profile. One advantage of this approach is that it creates a list of firms whose reputation, expertise, personality, and client base are already known to some members of the firm. It may also speed up the process. The approach, however, also has disadvantages, including a tendency to overlook many details of due diligence and a tendency for individual partners to identify deals that are self-serving, rather

19

than in the firm's best interest. In addition, if the candidate is ultimately not the right firm, partners may find it difficult to turn down people they know well.

◆ *Suggestions from clients.* Clients are often a good source of information on potential merger candidates. And having the support of a common client can also aid the business case.

◆ *Management consultants.* Consulting firms are a good source because they know the legal market well and may have relationships with firms that are good merger candidates.

◆ *Search firms.* A search firm may be a good source for individual lawyers or practice groups. Some search firms work on a retainer basis; however, many do not, and a law firm should understand the fee arrangement before hiring a search firm. Also, some search firms may focus more on completing a deal and earning their fee than on creating long-term value for both firms. Another key difference between a search firm and a management consulting firm is that the former typically will not have merger analysis and integration expertise.

◆ *Professional directories.* Directories such as *Martindale-Hubbell* can be used to develop a comprehensive list of possible firms. However, most of these directories are not detailed enough for determining whether a firm meets the profile. The firm usually ends up with a large list but without the qualitative information important to evaluating the potential fit. We have also found that managing partners and practice group leaders who are active in bar and other legal industry activities are more likely to have developed relationships with their peers at other firms. This not only increases the firm's knowledge of other firms but can help make the firm known in the marketplace as well.

Contacting Merger Prospects

Contacting merger prospects can be time-consuming and frustrating. First, there are the troublesome decisions of who should make the contacts and how it should be done. Some firms do not want other firms to know that they are looking for a merger, although that is less of an issue for most firms now that mergers are common, and firms of all sizes are at least considering the merger option as part of their strategic plan implementation. Confidentiality is difficult to maintain, and a firm may want to employ a third party to make the initial contact, with the understanding that the name of the firm will be released only with prior approval. This can be one of the roles of a management consultant or a search firm.

Before a firm actually begins a search for a suitable match, it must first decide whether it will initiate its own search or use the services of an outside organization.

The firm that initiates its own search has several advantages:

- ◆ Direct costs are lower.
- ◆ The firm is in control of the process.
- ◆ The firm knows its practice and client base intimately.
- ◆ The firm is in the best position to identify other lawyers with whom its members would enjoy practicing.

There are some disadvantages:

- ◆ It is likely to take an extraordinary amount of lawyer time and result in high intangible or *soft* costs—that is, costs that are not directly related to the merger process, especially loss of billable hours.
- ◆ The firm has little experience with the process.
- ◆ The firm may not be as objective as it needs to be in identifying a real, rather than a perceived, fit.
- ◆ The firm is not as likely to perform a widespread search.
- ◆ The firm is not as likely to be able to keep the momentum of the search moving and is more likely to be frustrated with being rejected.

There are a number of advantages to using an outside organization:

- ◆ An outside organization has been through the process many times and brings that experience to the situation.

- In some instances an outside organization may have existing relationships with the merger candidates.
- An outside organization can screen potential candidates, reducing unnecessary meetings.
- An outside party brings objectivity to the process.
- An outside party tends to be more realistic about the prospect of locating the firm's ideal candidate, particularly in other geographic areas.
- An outside party can help the firm prioritize the critical characteristics it seeks.
- An outside organization can help evaluate the two firms' fit.

The disadvantages of using an outside organization include:

- Higher direct cost, which, however, may actually be lower than the soft costs of lost lawyer time.
- The perception that an outside party cannot know the firm's practice as well as the firm itself does.

Communicating with Potential Merger Candidates

One partner or a very small group of partners should be designated as a search committee. Otherwise, the process may become disorganized and unfocused, which can result in many partners wasting time and energy. If the firm is working through an outside organization such as a management consultant, the consultant usually develops a game plan to determine how to initiate contact. It may be desirable for the consultant to make the first contact with firms on the list of potential merger candidates. Advantages of this approach are to save lawyer time and to initiate contact at the decision-making level.

The purpose of the initial communication is to assess the level of interest, if any, and to discuss each firm's practice and clients in broad terms. This initial discussion should help to confirm or disaffirm perceptions of the merger candidate's practice mix and client base. For example, does the firm's bankruptcy practice encompass debtor or creditor representation?

Once two firms have identified a mutual interest in pursuing merger, they should identify the partners in each firm who will coordinate the process. Unless the firms are extremely small, which would allow all partners to participate, a smaller group (often six or fewer) named as a merger committee is a more effective approach. The merger committee becomes the group in each firm responsible for accomplishing or calling off the merger. In many instances, each firm's executive committee serves as the merger committee. The responsibilities of the merger committee vary, depending on firm size, but typically include all aspects of coordinating the merger analysis and negotiating its terms.

The First Meeting

Once the firm has identified a prospective merger candidate that has expressed an interest, it is time to determine whether merger makes sense for both firms. This analysis is expensive and time-consuming, consisting of many steps. Both firms must exchange a great deal of financial and client data and other critical information relatively early in the process. This exchange must be well orchestrated. It is not necessary that all information be exchanged at the outset. Rather, there will be certain points in the process at which specific information must be shared.

Although economic issues are important, compatibility—including personalities and attitudes, firm culture, philosophies, and other people issues—is more likely to affect the merger decision. Do members of each firm think they would enjoy practicing with each other? Do they want the same things from the practice? Do they have a common vision for the combined firm? Merger evaluation is not so much a scientific measurement of whether the merger makes sense as it is a culmination of a process that results in a feeling among the partners that the merger will benefit both firms.

The first meeting is one of many get-acquainted meetings that the groups will have, assuming they decide to proceed with the discussions. The primary purpose of this meeting is to discuss the positive aspects of each firm and to determine whether there is enough surface compatibility to warrant further investigation; it is not a meeting to resolve potential issues. A small group of partners, either the merger committee or the executive committees of each group, typically attend the first meeting, which should last no more than three or four hours. Often this initial meeting is just between managing partners.

An agenda is essential for keeping the meeting moving and for ensuring that critical information is covered. Exhibit 2 (on page 126) is a sample agenda for the first meeting. The sample agenda is somewhat ambitious, and it may not be possible, or necessary, to discuss all items on the agenda at the first meeting. How much can be accomplished at this meeting will depend on whether the firms have any knowledge of each other and how much they have in common.

Some firms find that it takes more than one "first" meeting to determine whether it makes sense to go to the next step. The first meeting is more of a concept than a specific allocation of time. Often firms determine that a somewhat broader group may need to be involved before they are in a position to make an initial go/no-go decision. It could also take more than one meeting just to get through the high-level concepts. So don't be alarmed if after one meeting you don't feel that you have enough knowledge to make a decision.

The Next Step

Once the firms decide that they will explore further the possibility of merger, many additional meetings will be required. How many meetings are needed depends on the number of issues that must be resolved, the difficulty of resolving them, firm size, and the amount of time it takes partners in the firms to become comfortable with one another. If the first meeting is positive and the two merger committees feel that they are compatible with each other, they should begin to involve other partners. In small firms particularly, if not all partners are aware of the discussions, they should be told after the first meeting of the merger committees. In large firms, the process might not involve all partners until later. However, even in large firms, the circle of partners who become involved widens once the merger committee has decided to proceed beyond a first meeting.

If the two firms agree to go beyond the first meeting, they should begin to exchange information. The compatibility test includes four major areas: people, practice, clients, and economics.

The Strategic Merger Checklist

After the first meeting, it is important that both firms exchange certain information. There is no right or wrong way to structure the exchange of information or the order in which issues are addressed, as long as there is a willing and mutual exchange of needed information.

Before the exchange and analysis, the merger committee should prepare a strategic merger checklist and timetable that itemizes the activities and the schedule of their occurrence. See Exhibits 3 and 4 (pages 127–133) for samples. The checklist and timetable should serve only as a guide. Negotiations may require a deviation from the order of events, and the firms must be flexible. The firms should agree on the checklist as soon as possible after the first meeting. At this point the two firms normally agree that they will not have discussions with other firms during negotiations. Neither firm should undertake negotiations until both have made a commitment to each other.

Managing Internal and External Communications

Communication is key to developing support at every level of the firm. It is very difficult to keep merger discussions confidential, especially once the firms begin meeting. Partners cannot keep a secret, and the news of talks, even initial visits, will leak. We have found that the best time for communicating to partners is before the process even starts. Partners should fully buy in to the concept of merger before the firm's management begins to meet with firms. Management does not need to share the list of target firms with all partners but certainly should share what the ideal criteria are. News of a merger meeting should not come as a complete surprise to the partners of the firm.

Management should inform the partners, associates, paralegals, and staff in an organized way. Lawyers and staff get the wrong message when they learn about merger discussions outside the firm rather than from their own management group. Associates, paralegals, and staff will ask the same question: "What does merger mean for me?" Headhunters may call associates in the firm and use the possible merger as the reason the associates should flee to a more stable environment. Paralegals and staff will leave if they perceive or suspect that there may be some consolidation. The timing of these communications is tricky, and there are no hard-and-fast rules.

A word of caution: Be careful with written communications, because in this age you must always assume that internal written communications can quickly become external communications. Many firms have found meetings or conference calls a more effective means of communication.

Once the firm's employees are aware of merger discussions, management should keep them informed about the progress. Firm management needs to anticipate questions and be prepared to answer them.

Many mergers are newsworthy items. Management must make it clear to all firm lawyers and staff that the merger negotiations should not be discussed with anyone outside the two firms until the merger is completed. If a merger is particularly newsworthy, the firms must be prepared for leaks and may want to designate one lawyer from each firm as the media contact. When a leak happens, management response must be quick and decisive. Some firms hire a media consultant at the onset of discussions or appoint a strong in-house marketing person to work with the merger team. However, it is also important that the merger discussions not be pressured or driven by the media. Only a few mergers have been newsworthy enough that they have warranted more than a short story before being announced.

It is important, once discussions become public, to make sure that key clients are aware of the talks and the strategic reasons for the merger. Usually this is best done in face-to-face meetings.

Working with Outside Consultants and Other Advisors

While many firms have handled merger analysis without outside help and have done quite well, particularly if it is a second or third merger, others have found the process frustrating and time-consuming. The merger process is very complex, and some firms simply do not have the internal resources or the knowledge and experience needed to handle it. Law firm mergers are significantly different from corporate mergers because law firm mergers are people intensive. A corporate lawyer who handles mergers for clients may not be the right person to handle the merger of his or her own firm. A typical board of directors is less personally involved with a corporation than partners are with a law firm; a merger will directly affect the lives of the partners of a merging firm to a degree not experienced by board members. Since the board of directors is a small group, conflicts are more easily managed. The partners of a law firm compose a sizable constituency whose sometimes conflicting needs must be carefully considered. Because of the complexity of the many issues that must be addressed in merger discussions and negotiations, many firms retain the services of experienced management consultants, accountants, and even outside counsel to advise them during the merger. In addition, other professionals such as tax accountants, technology consultants, actuaries, and benefits consultants may be needed during the course of the discussions.

The firms realize a number of benefits when working with a consultant to analyze a prospective merger:

◆ *Analysis of economics.* A consultant or accountant can conduct a preliminary analysis of the economics of each firm without the firms having to share confidential data at an early stage. When the consultant has completed the financial review, the two firms and the consultant review the findings. The firms need not exchange detailed information until a full due diligence is required.

◆ *Business case.* A consultant can provide an objective appraisal of each firm's position in the market, as well as an assessment of the competitive position the combined firm would occupy. They can help the lawyers think through the strategic imperatives for the merger.

◆ *Experience.* A consultant has experience in evaluating mergers across a wide spectrum of firms. This experience enables the consultant to keep the process moving and ensure that issues are addressed when they should be. The consultant can also bring creative solutions to the issues that arise.

Of course, it is important to choose a consultant or other outside advisor who has experience with putting together successful law firm mergers.

Evaluating the Merger

4

Introduction

Because it is impossible to identify a typical sequence of events in a law firm merger, the following discussion is a representative approach. Mergers evolve in stages and require active participation by both firms over an extended period of time. There are no shortcuts. It is important for the two firms to develop confidence in, and a high level of comfort with, each other. Many lawyers do not realize that successfully evaluating, negotiating, and structuring a merger can be quite time-consuming. Throughout the analysis process, each firm must remain focused on the strategic reasons for pursuing the combination. Unless the merger gives each firm what each is looking for, it may not make sense, even if the firms meet the analysis and compatibility tests. Not surprisingly, only a small percentage of merger negotiations result in an actual merger.

Merger discussions and negotiations are different from the typical negotiations that lawyers undertake on behalf of their clients. In a law firm merger, the parties negotiating will become partners. There can be no winners or losers. It is critical to avoid a situation in which either merger candidate feels at a disadvantage. The firms must compromise significantly to consummate a merger. If one firm comes into the discussion with the attitude that its systems, policies, and procedures are better and is unwilling to consider alternatives, resolving the key merger issues will be virtually impossible. Firm practices will likely change as a result of the merger, and what has worked for an individual firm in the past may not necessarily work best for the combined firm. In fact, in most mergers, the constituent firms look for the opportunity to create a better, stronger firm and see the merger as an opportunity to improve on past practices.

Potential failures may be avoided with proper planning, thorough and honest evaluation, and in some cases, use of outside professional help to keep the discussions on track. The sections that follow address the essential tools and means of evaluating a law firm merger.

The Merger Committee and Subcommittees

Regardless of its composition, the merger committee plays a major role in the discussion, evaluation, and ultimate recommendation to merge or not to merge. Exhibit 5 (pages 134–135) describes the responsibilities of the merger committee. The committee's role varies, depending on the size of the firms, whether the committee is reporting to other management groups, and the extent to which subcommittees are used to work on the most difficult issues. The merger committee typically appoints subcommittees to deal with discrete topics. Some of these subcommittees will continue to function after the merger to help in the integration process. The following list gives examples of the types of subcommittees formed to deal with specific issues:

- ◆ *Finance.* See Exhibit 6 (page 136) for areas of responsibility.
- ◆ *Practice integration.* See Exhibit 7 (pages 137–138) for areas of responsibility, most of which go into effect after the decision to merge.

- *Conflicts.* See Exhibit 8 (page 139) for areas of responsibility.
- *Retirement and benefits.* See Exhibit 9 (page 140) for areas of responsibility.
- *Business development and marketing.* See Exhibit 10 (pages 141–142) for areas of responsibility, most of which go into effect after the decision to merge.
- *Associates/paralegals.* See Exhibit 11 (pages 143–144) for areas of responsibility, most of which go into effect after the decision to merge.

The larger the firms, the more they need subcommittees. In small firms, too many committees may be cumbersome, so the merger committee would deal with most, if not all, issues.

Many firms fall into the trap of selecting large subcommittees. The subcommittees should be small—no larger than three to four members from each firm. They are working rather than decision-making committees. Individuals whose leadership, vision, skills, and respect make them the best choice for the assignment should be asked to serve on the subcommittee. The subcommittees need not represent all practices, viewpoints, and age groups. If the subcommittee members do a competent job, they will solicit input from members throughout the firm on the issues being addressed.

The subcommittees cannot discuss each issue with all partners. A town meeting approach at every step of the way is often unsuccessful and will bring the process to a halt. Instead, the subcommittees should build consensus within their respective groups and then present their proposed resolutions to assorted issues to the partners during regularly held meetings.

Meetings

During the course of the merger, the merger committee and subcommittees will meet numerous times. These meetings are likely to combine social events held specifically to give the members an opportunity to meet each other with working sessions to resolve the various issues.

In addition to merger committee and subcommittee meetings, key (if not all) partners of the various practice areas should meet to get to know one another and evaluate potential merger synergy. A significant goal of the practice group meetings is to ensure that the partners in each firm accept one another both professionally and personally.

The number of meetings needed depends on firm size and the number and complexity of issues to be resolved. Issue resolution normally takes less time in small firms. Size, however, does not always indicate the amount of time needed to resolve major issues.

Well-planned meeting agendas and meetings that begin with a review of progress to date help firms stay on track and keep negotiations moving forward. The merger committee should also keep partners informed of progress through periodic reports. Since mergers can take many months to complete, it is important to maintain momentum and keep partners excited about the merger. If the discussions go on too long or if the gaps between meeting dates are too long, momentum can dissipate, and a merger that might otherwise have taken place falters.

Law firms evaluating a merger must spend the time necessary to deal with the issues that determine whether a merger will be successful. If the philosophies, personalities, and lifestyles of the lawyers differ, even though these differences may counterbalance one another, they may also create problems that will prevent the firms from integrating and the merger from succeeding.

Partners and associates may fear instability, change, and the unknown. They may feel insecure about their roles in the new firm. They may feel betrayed by the old firm and threatened by the new. They may resent allowing someone else to tell them how to spend their money and how to behave, as well as the need to prove themselves to strangers. They may worry about their chances of becoming partners. They may resent someone else setting their compensation. They may worry about others "stealing" their clients. If either firm fails to deal with the people issues during all stages of the merger process, the result will be disastrous.

One of the keys to integrating associates successfully in any merger is early, open communication usually once the business case for the merger has been established. Firms are also well advised to solicit the opinions of associates as the negotiations progress. Many partners are surprised at how flexible their associates are, even when a prospective merger may bring about changes to an associate's timetable for partnership consideration.

Major Issues

Firms must work through numerous, diverse issues throughout the merger evaluation process. Most can usually be resolved. Others may break up the deal. The significance of the issues varies dramatically from merger to merger. The partners in each firm must know how the various issues should affect their decision to merge and how the issues will affect the merger's success.

Firm Name

In practically every merger, the choice of name for the new firm is a sensitive issue. In some states, ethical guidelines may restrict the choices. It is preferable to resolve this issue relatively early, since the firm's name can be one of the most sensitive issues to resolve and can kill a deal. Devoting energy to other aspects of the analysis before dealing with the name can be a waste of time. In some instances, however, if the firms have identified a number of reasons why the merger should proceed, discussion of the name can be postponed. The hope is that as the partners get to know each other better, see the potential benefits of the merger, and resolve other issues, the name issue will resolve itself. The name is less of an issue when a large firm is acquiring a small firm or practice group.

It is difficult to generalize about how to reach a decision on name. Some lawyers place an inflated value on a name. If a partner's name has been in the firm's name and may be dropped as a result of the merger, the partner's ego may be difficult to placate. Nonetheless, the name should not be changed to satisfy an individual's ego and allay the insecurity of a particular partner. Marketing, reputation, and continuity should be the determinants for selecting the firm's name. In some of the largest mergers, public relations consultants have been retained to test market name options.

One useful technique is to have the merger committee list various options for the combined firm's name. When the list has been narrowed to a few names, the final name can be selected from a business development and marketing standpoint, since that is the primary reason for most mergers. Since the partners in each firm usually approve the name, the merger committee must build consensus among the partners for the proposed name.

In some mergers, the combined firm has taken on a transitional name in specific locations where one of the predecessor firms was a dominant player. The transitional name is typically a combination of the two firms' names and is used for a short period (one to three years) before a single firmwide identity is adopted. In practice, we often find that the constituent firms agree to use a transitional name for a fixed period of time but find it cumbersome and move to a unified firm name well before the planned expiration of the transitional name period.

Conflicts

Once a business case for the merger has been established, firms should share complete client lists so that they can determine whether conflicts of interest exist. Initially, the firms are simply ensuring that there are no significant conflicts. Of course, the search for potential conflicts should continue throughout the discussions, as additional conflicts may surface in new work for existing clients or work from new clients.

The conflicts check should include both client and business conflicts. A check for direct client conflicts is the traditional review that most firms perform as part of their normal practice. Checking business conflicts is much more difficult because it involves an assessment of the types of legal matters the firms handle, the types of clients they represent, and how that representation may affect the interests of other clients.

If the firms identify a direct conflict of interest between major clients representing significant revenues to one or both firms, the course of action is generally clear. In fact, this type of direct client conflict frequently brings merger discussions to an abrupt, amicable end. In some instances, however, the two firms postpone discussions until the conflict is resolved through completion of the matter causing the conflict. Some client conflicts can be resolved by giving up certain clients, especially if the clients do not represent significant revenues to the firm. There are also situations in which the clients may be willing to waive the conflict. Of course, this necessitates discussions with the clients. It is difficult to say when clients should be consulted about conflicts. The timing is dictated by when the responsible partner is comfortable approaching the client to discuss the prospective merger.

Business conflicts typically occur within practice areas. For example, one firm may represent labor, and the other management. One firm may represent plaintiffs who litigate against major corporate clients of the other firm. One firm may represent creditors, while the other represents debtors. The interests of some clients may also be contrary to the interests of other clients who would be added in a merger. This is particularly problematic in competitive consolidating industries with a few key players. A significant factor to consider is whether any key clients would look elsewhere for services as a result of a merger; therefore, it is important to know how key clients feel about the merger candidate.

An examination of referral business also is important, since the combined firm may not always depend on a continuing source of referrals after a merger. This area is not always examined as carefully as it should be and can have a devastating effect on a merger. This is particularly true if the firm is a highly specialized one that receives much of its work from other law firms. For example, a small employment practice may lose a substantial amount of its referral business if it merges with a larger, full-service firm. It is important to evaluate the source of referrals and whether the referrals would continue after a merger.

Economics

Merging two financially strong firms presents the greatest opportunity for economic success. Few successful mergers have come from a strong firm merging with a significantly weaker one. Merging two weak firms can result in economic disaster, as the two weak firms tend to drag each other down. Economic analysis is a critical component of the merger evaluation. (See Chapter 5.) The analysis should always include the development of an economic balance sheet and pro forma projections of financial performance. (See Chapters 6 and 7.)

A number of economic issues must be resolved including:

- *Accounts receivable.* Will the accounts receivable of each firm be pooled for the benefit of both firms? Do any tax consequences arise?
- *Work in progress.* Will the work in progress at the time of the merger be pooled? If one of the firms has certain matters on which substantial fees for work done in the past might be received (e.g., long-standing contingent matters), will everyone share in that fee when it is received, or will a schedule of excluded fees be established?
- *Billing and collection practices.* One firm may have a policy of billing most matters monthly, and the other firm may have a more erratic policy, with some billing done semiannually, annually, or upon completion. Pro forma projections should reflect the firms' best estimate of the timing and amount of cash flow. (See Chapter 6.)
- *Office lease and leasehold improvements.* The analysis must include a review of each firm's lease agreement as well as any sublease options or arrangements. Space issues include office expansion options, lease terms, an assessment of pass-through costs, and a valuation of space cost versus the marketplace. Who will pay for the rent if a leasehold obligation is to be assumed, and how will the payment be handled? If the merger results in only one office, is there adequate space to house both firms? If two offices are consolidated, what is the tax effect of writing off leasehold improvements? Has a projection been made for space requirements for the next five years? If so, will the present space or existing options handle the requirements? Is subleasing permitted?

◆ *Professional liability insurance.* Since most policies are for claims made, a major issue is providing prior acts coverage for one of the firms. Sometimes this cost is added to the regular (ongoing) insurance premiums and allocated to both firms ratably. An important exchange between the firms is the sharing of each firm's claims history and information regarding the possibility and magnitude of any future claims. Depending on the deductibles of one or both firms, it may be appropriate to consider a contingency reserve. A philosophic decision is the policy deductible and aggregate claims limits. An examination of the client base and practice areas provides information to help make the decision. The question is one of cost versus risk management.

◆ *Unrecorded liabilities.* Since most law firms maintain their accounting records on a cash basis, each firm is likely to have unrecorded liabilities. These can include normal trade accounts payable, operating leases, and amounts due to former and current partners for partially or fully unfunded retirement and other withdrawal benefits. Each item needs to be evaluated. (See Chapter 7.)

◆ *Capital structure.* What capital requirements will the new entity have? How will the firm generate working capital? Some firms do not require capital contributions from new partners. Others require substantial amounts. Some take notes from the partners, and others require that partners make outside arrangements (possibly guaranteed by the firm). Different approaches in capital requirements and payment for capital requirements must be resolved. How will the firm finance long-term capital needs? Will the partners be asked to contribute more capital to the firm? What is the firm's borrowing philosophy? What level of debt can the firm support (or afford)? How will the firm use long-term and short-term borrowing?

◆ *Fiscal year.* What are the problems associated with different fiscal years? Although it may be desirable to have a fiscal year rather than a calendar year, would a fiscal year

create a "bunching of income" problem? This is much less
an issue today in the United States, since most U.S. firms
are now operating on a calendar year.

♦ *Tax consequences.* Will there be tax consequences as a result of the structure of the combined firm (i.e., corporation
into corporation, partnership into partnership, partnership into corporation, or two entities forming a new, third
entity)? The tax treatment varies depending on the merged
firm's structure, and if the merger is not handled properly,
it could result in unfavorable tax consequences. Tax issues
may also arise as a result of the firms' depreciating fixed
assets on different bases. When the assets are combined,
establishing a value for contributing assets will also affect
credit given to partners for capital.

Partner Compensation

The partner compensation approach can tell the firms a great deal
about their respective cultures and philosophies. A useful tool in
identifying the differences in compensation philosophies is to compare the two systems side by side. (See Exhibit 12 on page 145.)
There is no question that a firm's compensation system influences
the behavior of partners, particularly in practice management issues. For example, a compensation system that overemphasizes
personal production may produce a situation in which associates
are underproductive because partners hoard work to improve
their own statistics; a compensation system with a significant seniority element may mean that partners have little accountability
for their practice management behavior.

The two extremes in partner compensation systems are for-
mulas and subjective approaches. These extremes represent a serious difference in philosophies that can be difficult to resolve. The
firms' compensation philosophies must be discussed to determine
if they are compatible or could be made compatible. At what level
will the partners be compensated after the merger takes effect?
What guarantees, if any, either implied or otherwise, will be made
by the partners in one firm to those of the other? This issue must

be completely worked out in writing before any merger becomes final.

It is not unusual to work out a transitional approach for the first year or two. The goal is to get both firms on one system as soon as possible so that they feel and behave as if they are one firm. (See Chapter 9.)

It is also not unusual for the combined firm to implement a different compensation system after the merger. However, a new compensation system cannot be designed in a vacuum. The merged firm's compensation system must consider the goals of the merged firm and must support implementation of its goals. The system, which should be in writing, should include these components:

- An articulation of the firm's philosophy and goals. The writing would include a recitation not only of what the system is designed to reward and penalize but also how the criteria are analyzed and weighted.
- Criteria for evaluating partner performance and the period of time covered by the evaluation (i.e., one year, three years, five years).
- How draws will be set.
- Whether there will be a bonus component of the system.
- Whether the management group or a separate compensation committee will set compensation. If there is a separate committee, how will the committee be elected, and what term will it serve?
- How often compensation will be set (e.g., annually, biannually) and when it will be set.
- How partners will be held accountable.
- The mechanics of the system and how partners are involved in the process.

Retirement, Voluntary Withdrawal, Expulsion, Disability, and Death Benefits

Retirement, voluntary withdrawal, expulsion, disability, and death benefits are discussed in detail in Chapter 5 because they can have significant economic bearing on merger discussions. These issues, however, are not purely economic ones. They are cultural and philosophical as well. Because of their long-term economic and cultural implications, policies that vary widely can be deal breakers.

Benefits paid to withdrawing partners (whether for death, disability, retirement, voluntary withdrawal, or expulsion) are deferred compensation, although they are sometimes described as buyouts. The amounts of these benefits, as well as how they are paid, vary widely. Buy-in policies also affect these issues, especially if new partners "buy into" work in progress and accounts receivable.

In merger discussions, problems can arise when the firms are at philosophical extremes, as in the following example:

- ◆ Firm 1 pays no additional compensation benefit to a withdrawing partner; a withdrawing partner would get back his or her paid-in capital (after-tax dollars contributed to the firm) and current year undistributed earnings and would receive any money he or she had accumulated in a portable pension or profit-sharing plan.
- ◆ Firm 2 pays a specified benefit based on the partner's compensation or an interest in accounts receivable and work in progress; the benefit may or may not be funded.

Partners who are accustomed to funded benefits will not want to lose them and may be unwilling to contribute current earnings to fund an obligation brought by the firm with a partially funded or unfunded plan. Unfunded benefits can present a significant enough economic problem to break an otherwise sound deal. (See Chapter 5.) However, as more firms eliminate or reduce unfunded plans, this will become less of a barrier. Some firms have even used the merger as an opportunity to address their existing unfunded commitment to partners.

Policies on partner expulsion and retirement also fall into this category of issues. For example, in some firms partners can be expelled only for cause, but in other firms expulsion can be without cause. Some firms provide for mandatory retirement with a phasedown period, while others have no retirement policy at all. As these issues cannot be resolved after merging, the firms must have an agreement in principle before the merger.

Management Structure

The management structure of each firm is another important cultural issue. Partners in most large firms have long been accustomed to centralized management. Partners in small and midsize firms may not be. Although some firms have moved toward centralized management, many cling to a democratic approach to firm governance. A useful tool in examining the differences in management structures is to compare them side by side as shown in Exhibit 13 (page 146).

An in-depth analysis of a firm's partnership (or shareholder or operating) agreement can provide a wealth of information about the firm. For example, voting requirements on key issues show how democratic the firm may be. The partnership agreement may describe the system of governance, defining levels of responsibility and authority. The agreement may also define the compensation philosophy and system, as well as how the value of shares or percentage interests is determined and the basis for valuation. Of course, the partnership agreement does not tell the whole story, so each key issue must also be discussed.

Although establishment of the management structure for the combined firm rarely kills a merger, the level of lawyer involvement in management is a good indicator of a firm's culture and the likelihood that the firms are compatible enough to thrive together. Do the partners in the two firms trust each other enough to delegate substantial management responsibility to a small group? Will each firm have ample representation in management? If the partners are hesitant to delegate authority, they should seriously reconsider their decision to merge, since a larger firm necessarily means more delegation of authority.

The management structure must be agreed on and set in place before, not after, the merger. The firms must arrive at a policy on these categories:

- Which decisions will require partner approval, which decisions will require a simple majority vote, and which will require a supermajority vote. The bigger the firm, the fewer decisions are likely to be reserved for the partners.
- Whether voting will be per capita, by compensation percentages, or by a combination of the two on some votes.
- Whether the new firm will have only a managing partner, a management committee, or both.
- How the managing partner will be elected or appointed, term of office, responsibilities, authority, and accountability.
- How the management committee will be elected, representation of both firms, terms of office, reelection guidelines, responsibilities, authority, and accountability.
- Whether compensation will be set by a separate committee or by the management committee.
- Departmental structure and the responsibilities, authority, and reporting lines of department and/or practice group heads.
- The administrative structure and the responsibilities, authority, and reporting lines of administrative staff.

The structure may be transitional and may result in a larger than normal management committee for the first two to three years. It is not unusual in mergers of any size to mandate representation from each firm for a specified time, usually two years or less. If one of the merging firms is small, the structure will probably vary, and the management group is usually smaller. The management structure, including decisions reserved to the partners and duties of the management committee, should be included in the merger agreement and ultimately in the new partnership agreement.

Practice Compatibility

Aside from the pure economic and cultural issues, two significant factors in determining synergy are practice expertise and client base. A key aspect of the practice analysis should be an assessment of the market position of the combined firm's practice. The threshold question should be, Will the merger enhance competitiveness?

The examination process should include review of client lists by practice area and also by originating or responsible lawyer. The practice area list should indicate the types of clients being served, the nature of the services being performed, the dollar volume of work, and the potential for cross-selling opportunities. The client list generated by the originating or responsible lawyer will provide information about who the key players are and which lawyers will have to be involved in identifying and planning the cross-selling opportunities. The following list has some important topics in evaluating key clients.

- What percentage of revenue is accounted for by the top client as well as the top five, ten, twenty, and fifty clients of each firm? (This question is also asked as part of the financial analysis.)
- How many dollars in fees have the top clients paid during the past few years? What are the trends?
- How many of the top clients have remained top clients through the years?
- Which partners "control" the top clients?
- In what industries are the top clients?
- Have the clients been cross-sold effectively? What cross-selling opportunities will result from the merger?
- What additional business does each firm hope to get from the top clients?
- What is the nature of service being provided to existing clients?
- What is the nature of the client relationship, and how frequently does each client send business?
- What is the quality of the relationship? Is the client loyal to the institution or only to the responsible lawyer?
- Is the client comfortable with the idea of the merger with the other firm?

- Is there anything about the other firm that is a problem for the client?
- Is there any possibility for additional work, either in the same practice area or in others, becoming available as a result of the merger?

Once serious merger discussions are under way, client managers must begin to contact key clients. The list of clients being contacted must expand as the discussions are drawing the firms nearer to merger. The merger announcement should not surprise most clients.

Practice Philosophies and Policies

The practice philosophies of the two firms are a significant factor in evaluating cultural compatibility. Each firm's philosophies in each of the following areas should be discussed early in the merger talks:

- *Department structure.* Some firms organize their practices by area of expertise (litigation, tax, real estate, etc.), some by industry group (banking, energy, health, etc.), and some by clients or by a combination of these. If the two firms organize their practices differently, the merger committee or practice integration subcommittee must identify those differences so the firms can determine how best to integrate their practices. It is a mistake to have both firms continue to practice under different structures in the merged firm, because it will be difficult to capitalize on opportunities. (See Exhibit 14 on page 147 for a side-by-side comparison to identify differences.)
- *Specialization.* Since a majority of lawyers now specialize, specialization may not be as much of an issue as it once was, especially in large firms. In small and midsize firms, however, it is not unusual to find lawyers who do not specialize, either because they prefer to be general practitioners or because the firm's compensation system inhibits specialization. If one firm is composed of specialists and

the other of general practitioners, or a significant number of them, a merger may be difficult to implement.

◆ *Work/client intake.* Some firms have learned to be selective in the kinds of work they accept, while others take anything and everything that comes through the door. Some firms have written guidelines; others do not. Some of the questions that must be discussed are: Does acceptance of work require approval, or can a partner or associate unilaterally accept business? Are fee letters and retainer arrangements required? Is a credit check performed on new clients? What types of fee arrangements are accepted? Do the guidelines apply in all instances or only under certain circumstances? In addition to discussing work intake in evaluating compatibility, the firms should also agree on a philosophy for the combined firm.

◆ *Pricing, billing, and collection.* Some firms require that clients be billed monthly and that any write-downs from standard rates be approved. In other firms partners have total autonomy regarding these matters. The same is true of collection responsibility, stop-work policies for clients that do not pay, and other collection practices. All these policies must be discussed and agreed on before the merger.

◆ *Vertical and horizontal delegation, staffing, and work assignment.* In some firms partners have complete autonomy about whether they will do the work themselves or delegate it to another partner or an associate. In such firms partners also typically assign work directly to whomever they would like to work with on the matter. Other firms have policies and guidelines on how work will be delegated, assigned, and staffed to ensure that work is handled at the appropriate level and that workloads are equalized to the extent possible. These issues must be addressed and resolved before the merger.

◆ *Cross-selling.* The merged firm should get significant cross-selling opportunities from the merger. To make recommendations regarding opportunities for the new firm, the merger committee or business development and marketing subcommittee must examine the level of cross-selling currently being done in each firm, the methodology for doing the cross-selling, and the extent to which it is being done. If there is a significant difference between the firms' levels of cross-selling, the committee or subcommittee should recommend ways to raise the awareness of the need to market and to involve all firm lawyers in cross-selling.

◆ *Use of client teams from various practice disciplines.* Some firms designate teams of lawyers with specific expertise in practice areas to respond to client needs. If this approach is used in either of the firms, the committee must develop a procedure for implementing a similar approach in the merged firm.

◆ *Getting the work out.* The firms must agree on how the merged firm will manage client relationships, an area that is critical to a merged firm's ability to market and cross-sell. Some firms believe that the client is better served using a cost-benefit approach. They discuss with the client up front what the costs and benefits of various approaches will be. This gives the client greater control over the project plan.

One difficulty may be partners' attitudes toward institutionalization of clients. Often the individual partners regard clients as their own or as clients of the former firm, rather than as clients of the new entity. They prefer to use personnel from their old firm to service those clients. Unless a real effort is made to integrate the clients, the result will be two firms rather than one.

◆ *Quality control systems.* These include audit and opinion letters, docket, conflicts, retrieval systems, and other written procedures and guides that help with quality control. Some firms have centralized quality control systems and procedures, while others leave quality control to individual lawyers. If the first kind of firm merges with the second, serious quality control problems may result if the merged firm is unable to get lawyers to comply with centralized procedures. It is especially important for a merged firm to be able to run effective conflicts of interest checks. If one of the firms has a centralized process for audit and opinion letters and the other firm does not, the two firms must agree on a common approach for the future.

◆ *Future growth and marketing.* Although it is not possible to develop a full business plan before the merger, it is important for both firms to articulate general plans for future expansion and the way the firm will be marketed.

Partner Policies

The level of partner perquisites and the degree of flexibility that partners have in their activities can vary widely. Because these are issues that can often affect the partners directly, they can cause more problems in the merger discussions than would otherwise be expected.

◆ *Expense reimbursement.* Conflicts often result when a firm that does not believe partners should have lavish expense accounts merges with one that believes that every expense possible should be charged through the firm. If this conflict is not resolved, each partner will be constantly looking over the shoulders of the other partners to see how much they are benefiting from their expense accounts. Even policies on reimbursement of bar dues can be an issue. It is also important to understand how these expenses are handled in order to view relative partner compensation levels accurately.

◆ *Outside activities.* Some firms encourage civic, charitable, and political activities and contributions. A firm that frowns on outside activities by its lawyers is courting danger in proposing a merger with a firm that encourages such activities unless this difference in concept can be resolved before the merger.

◆ *Investments.* Some firms make investments in their clients; others do not. Some firms own their own buildings; others stay away from all types of outside investments. Any differences must be resolved before the merger.

◆ *Vacation time, sabbaticals, parental leave, nepotism, and the like.* These are a matter of firm philosophy and vary a great deal from firm to firm. Each of these must be addressed and uniform policies developed for the merged firm.

Work Ethic

How hard people work or are willing to work is one of the most important characteristics of firm culture. Some firms have consciously chosen quality of life over earnings. In other firms partners want to maximize their earnings and are willing to work hard to do so. Some firms look for what they consider a reasonable balance. Of course, *reasonable balance* is a subjective phrase, so this topic bears discussion early in the analysis.

Although it is difficult to generalize about work ethic compatibility, if average billable and nonbillable hours for partners and associates for the past few years have been similar, this indicates that the work ethics are most likely compatible. A significant difference in hours recorded may reflect a vastly different culture. In some situations, fewer hours can mean a drop in work, rather than work ethic. Firms should compare hours worked and understand the reasons for any differences. Significantly different work ethics have caused numerous deals to fail.

Underproductive Partners

This issue is a potential deal breaker and, unfortunately, not one with an easy solution. Irrespective of merger, most firms have trouble dealing with the issue of underproductive partners. Having to deal with the problem in merger negotiations is less than ideal. Nevertheless, if a firm has not resolved this problem, it must do so now.

It is the merger committee's responsibility to identify why a lawyer is underproductive. Answering the following questions helps:

◆ Is the partner simply in a practice area where work is slow? One solution may be to devote the necessary time and effort to help the lawyer build a new practice specialty.

◆ Is the partner unwilling to work as much as others in the firm? If this is the case, one solution may be to exclude that partner from the merged firm. Another solution may be a change in partner status.

◆ Has the partner not kept pace with developments in the field? Has the partner continued to be a general practitioner without a specialty? Assuming quality of work is not a problem, this lawyer might be included in the merger but not as an equity partner. Another solution is not to include the partner.

◆ Are partners hesitant to refer work to this partner because of poor work quality? In this situation, the partner should be told that the merger will not include him or her.

◆ Are partners hesitant to refer work to this partner because of his or her inability to deal with clients effectively? If so, this partner should be told that the merger will not include him or her. Some groups might try to keep such a partner by changing the partner's compensation and status (becoming an income partner or of counsel), but this could be a divisive solution.

◆ Are partners hesitant to refer work to this partner because of his or her billing and collection practices? If so, this behavior could mean a different practice philosophy, and this partner doesn't belong in his or her current firm, much less a merged one.

◆ Is the partner a problem because of his or her personality or difficult work habits, such as a solo practitioner mentality? Whether or not this partner would be excluded from the merger depends on the severity of the problem, whether members of the firm have discussed it with the partner before, and whether the partner is willing to address the issue.

The merger committee should have honest discussions about problem partners. If one or more partners will not be invited into the merged firm, management of the respective firms should deal with them outside the merger. Waiting until after the merger has been accomplished can create low morale and divisiveness, and it may delay integration.

Firm Structure

The merger committee must consider the variety of legal structures available: partnership, limited liability partnership, professional corporation, professional association, professional limited liability corporation, and corporation. The committee must analyze the tax ramifications and the effect on existing retirement plans. Frequently, merging firms retain an accounting firm to address these tax issues.

Analysis of firm structure must also include a discussion of various classifications for lawyers, such as income partners, contract lawyers, staff lawyers, permanent associates, and their statuses. Typically, the merged firm does not create new classes at the time of the merger. The need for additional classes of lawyers is usually analyzed after the merger.

Determining the structure is relatively easy. What is not easy is the classification of lawyers at the effective date of the merger. For example, if the merged firm will have a two-tier structure, will all equity partners from each firm remain equity partners, or will some be reclassified as income partners? This is a major cultural and political issue beyond the scope of this book. While firms have merged successfully while transitioning pre-merger equity partners to a post-merger non-equity status, the difficulty in doing so and the possibility that the firm could lose partners who are unhappy about their change in status cannot be overestimated.

Associate Management

Although most associate issues can be satisfactorily resolved, the merger analysis should address the two firms' philosophies about associate management. Too often, firms assume that the associates will just naturally fit together with few problems. The truth is that a merger can be seriously impaired, or even destroyed, by lack of adequate communication and planning for associate development and management.

Every merger analysis should include some basic questions about the management of associates. For example, where do associates get their work? Are associates assigned to individual lawyers, or do they receive work assignments from a team of partners or all of the partners in the practice group or department? What are the billable hour requirements for associates? Is each associate expected to fulfill certain nonbillable requirements? What types of nonbillable activities are encouraged? These questions are especially important in a merger between two firms of drastically different sizes, since the work environment and working relationships of associates from the smaller firm are likely to change drastically.

Other Associate Issues

A few additional associate issues are important:

- ◆ *Recruiting.* The merger committee should review the basic recruiting philosophies of each firm. How active is each firm in its recruiting efforts? How and where are those recruiting efforts being directed? Do both firms recruit first-year lawyers? Does one of the firms recruit laterally only? It is increasingly common for firms to have only minimal recruiting programs, relying instead on lateral hires and acquisitions. How the merged firm will pursue its recruiting efforts should be discussed and decided before the merger is final. In addition, the merger committee must decide if the existing recruiting efforts should be continued as planned or whether the merger itself will provide the necessary resources for the upcoming year.

  An often-overlooked aspect of any basic recruiting program is the summer clerk program. Some firms spend large sums of money recruiting, entertaining, and assessing their summer clerks, while others skip the process entirely and rely solely on law school interviews.

◆ *Training and supervision.* These are important to any firm's future but tend to vary tremendously. Formal training programs are not usually possible in small firms, but some small and midsize firms do use training checklists of assignments to ensure that associates get exposure to a broad range of work. In some firms, associates learn through their work, but this approach can vary significantly. An associate may be involved in a file from beginning to end or may be trained by working on only parts of a file.

Some firms assign new associates to a mentor to help the new lawyer become oriented to the firm and become a good lawyer. Some firms provide associates with excellent supervision; other firms provide little. These issues must be addressed to develop a uniform approach for the merged firm.

◆ *Evaluation and compensation.* The frequency, method, and management of associate evaluations should be discussed and agreed on before the merger.

One important consideration in any merger is how the associates' salaries will be integrated. It is not unusual to find that the firms have dissimilar compensation and benefits packages. Some merged firms are tempted to leave the salary differences in place, but this information quickly leaks out, creating unnecessary dissension and turnover that is far more expensive than integrating the salary levels.

◆ *Promotion.* A number of issues involving promotion to partnership must be examined: track to partnership, existing commitments to associates, criteria for becoming a partner, admission of new partners, and associate classifications. Most firms have discovered that they cannot commit to a guaranteed partnership track. They try to maintain their commitments to associates for first consideration at a given time but announce that the track may be extended from time to time to keep pace with the economics of running a law firm. Many merged firms have difficulty deciding how they will assess merged associates who are coming up for partnership. In many cases this issue is resolved by leaving partnership decisions for the first year with the partners from the respective firm. In most successful mergers, the firm continues to observe any definite commitments for partnership made before the merger.

Multitier partnerships and other alternatives to equity partnership have become a way of life. Many firms that have not yet changed their structures to accommodate this trend are reexamining their structures as part of their planning.

Administration and Technology

Although these issues are unlikely to jeopardize the merger, each firm's administrative and technology systems must be analyzed to determine if either or both will work for the new firm or if new systems will be needed. The personnel and financial ramifications of these decisions can be significant, and a plan must be developed for the new firm. Decisions about systems and the cost of integration must also be considered in the merged firm's pro forma projections. (See Chapters 6 and 10.)

Part of the analysis process frequently overlooked is a comparison of firm policies and procedures. Each firm's office manual is a good place to start. However, the items covered in an office manual are typically more administrative and should be discussed much later in the process. (See Chapter 10.)

Historical Financial Analysis | 5

Introduction

Previous chapters addressed some of the issues that firms must evaluate long before they need a detailed economic analysis. Although a historical financial analysis can be helpful, it is a mistake to place too much emphasis on history. The economics can often be made to work, but if the firms have incompatible cultures and philosophies, the numbers alone will not make the merger successful. On the other hand, financial information not only helps in the analysis of the firms' economic compatibility, it can also help assess the cultures and philosophies of the two firms. Many economic issues tend to be cultural as well.

The most important element of the financial picture is the future: does the merger enhance the financial and market positions of the existing firms? In other words, will the combined firm attain professional and financial results that neither firm could reach on its own?

Lawyers tend to put too much emphasis on past performance and statistical analyses. It is only human for partners to be concerned about how the merger will affect them: "Am I going to be any better off as a result of merger? How much is it going to cost me to do a merger?" For the merger to be successful, the majority of partners must see that they will be better off in the long term (although not necessarily in the short term) than if they had not merged.

Census Data and Demographics

The basis for many of the tests in a financial analysis is a weighted average (full-time equivalent) calculation of the number of lawyers in the firm during the year. That figure is the foundation for per-lawyer and per-partner calculations, such as revenue per lawyer, expenses and overhead per lawyer, net income per partner, and average billable hours. For the historical analysis to be useful, accurate census information is essential.

Accurate dates of hire and termination are critical to the calculation of weighted average statistics. For example, a lawyer or paralegal beginning employment on July 1 is considered as 0.50 for calculating weighted averages. Also, lawyers changing status (e.g., associate to partner) should be included in the averages of both timekeeper classes for the time at each level during the year. Lawyers or paralegals that leave the firm during the course of the year should be counted only for the period of time when they were with the firm.

While the weighted average statistics are critical to the financial analysis, the data used to develop the averages can give some clues of many noneconomic considerations that must be taken into account in a merger. Here are examples:

◆ If a firm has no partners over fifty years of age, does that mean the firm was formed as a result of a spin-off from another firm? If so, what caused the split? Could the cause surface in the merged firm?

◆ If partners are in their sixties and forties and younger, with virtually no one in the middle, what happened to the middle group? What steps are being taken to ensure a transition from the senior partners to the younger partners in terms of client responsibility and management? Is younger leadership being groomed?

◆ Turnover of lawyers or paralegals during the past three years may be an indication of the firm's stability or lack of it. It is important to determine the reasons for departures, including whether the firm lost significant clients as a result of departures.

Benchmarks for Economic Evaluation

To measure economic compatibility and identify economic trends effectively, it is helpful to compare not less than three years' historical performance plus the current-year budget. (The information needed for this comparison is listed in Exhibit 15 on pages 148–152.) The typical approach to testing the economic compatibility of the two firms is to analyze and compare the following benchmarks:

1. Fee revenue per equity partner.
2. Fee revenue per lawyer.
3. Net income per partner and partner compensation, split by compensation bands (e.g., x partners earned between $200,000 and $275,000).
4. Expenses and overhead per lawyer.
5. Leverage and staff ratios.
6. Billable and nonbillable hour averages.
7. Hourly (standard) billing rates.
8. Realization rates for billing and collections (calculated using standard rates).
9. Work in progress, accounts receivable, and inventory aging and turnover.
10. Collections from top clients (e.g., percent of total fees received from top client, top five, top ten, top twenty, top fifty).

11. Capitalization.
12. Valuation of assets.
13. Liabilities (on and off balance sheet).
14. Retirement, withdrawal, disability, and death benefits.
15. Compensation of income/non-equity partners and associates.

Although analysis of these benchmarks alone does not determine the potential long-term viability of a merger, the analysis serves several important functions:

- A similar economic picture raises the comfort level for both groups.
- The analysis depicts each firm's economic stability and performance trends.
- The tests give clues to each firm's culture and practice philosophies. While the tests alone cannot verify compatible cultures, they can support philosophies identified through the first impression. This type of verification lends another layer of comfort.
- On a more functional level, the various tests are valuable in developing financial projections for the merged entity.

Needless to say, the numbers themselves are not the most important aspect of the analysis. What is more important is their interpretation. Often, the financial analysis simply raises other questions and issues that must be discussed, resolved, and considered in projecting future performance for the merged entity. The economic analysis is most valuable in determining whether the numbers get in the way of doing the deal. Is there any item so glaring in the analysis, are the differences so great, that the merger cannot happen?

For easy comparison of two firms, it is best to align the previously listed key statistics in a side-by-side format. The critical factors must be comparable (apples to apples). Getting to the apples-to-apples comparison is more difficult than would be expected. Each revenue and expense item must be evaluated to ensure similar treatment. When comparing these statistics, ask: How are some of the differences accounted for? What creates these differences? Can the firms live with these differences? Can the differences be justified? How might those differences affect the merged entity's future performance? Analysis of the individual benchmarks listed below formulates a picture of each firm and determines how the firms may fit together in the future.

Fee Revenue per Equity Partner

When comparing the historical economic performance of two firms, it is important to review the firms' average fee revenue per equity partner. While the per-partner average will not shed light on the amount, or quality, of an individual partner's book of business, the average itself and the trend in the average may reveal a lot about a firm's criteria for reaching the equity level.

Fees per equity partner can decline because of an overall reduction in a firm's revenue base. On the other hand, such declines may indicate that the firm has promoted too many partners to the equity rank without requisite books of business (effectively diluting the average). While it may be unrealistic to expect that a new partner will have a book of business equal to the firm's average partner, a steep or steady declines in revenue per partner without corresponding drops in firm revenue may indicate that the firm's newest partners are generating little work on their own. In the end, this lowers revenue per partner and may lower net income per partner as the firm's income is split into more slices, although the size of the overall pie is largely unchanged.

In addition to reviewing the average statistics by partner, many firms also look at the average for specific subsets within the partner group. Most often, the average is recalculated based on specific ranges of years of experience, partner age, or practice area. By taking this extra step, firms can analyze the diversification of business generation by partner group.

Fee Revenue per Lawyer

Fee revenue per lawyer is a far more meaningful statistic than total gross revenues because it gives a more reasonable basis for comparison. Fee revenue per lawyer is computed by dividing the firm's gross fees by the number of full-year equivalent lawyers. Note that reimbursement of client costs should not be included in revenue for these calculations. Instead, these reimbursements should be accounted for as an offset to (reduction of) expenses.

All performance statistics are most valuable when tracked from year to year, because the long-term trend is more important than a one-year picture. The same holds true for fee revenue per lawyer. For example, a firm may show consistent increases in gross revenue each year. On a per-lawyer basis, however, revenue may actually be flat. This is not necessarily bad; it may indicate that the firm expanded the number of lawyers and there has been sufficient additional client business to support the growth. A decline in gross revenue per lawyer may indicate that the firm has expanded beyond its ability to produce enough work to keep additional lawyers busy, that the firm's realization, billing, and collection rates have declined, that it lost a key client, or a host of other reasons. A decrease in average gross revenue per lawyer is not necessarily cause for alarm, but it does raise questions about what is happening at the firm. The decline could be relatively innocuous. For example, it could be caused by increased leverage, which shifts the effective billing rate down, which is not necessarily a bad thing.

Net Income per Partner

Average net income per partner should be calculated for at least the past three years and the current year's budget. The method used in calculating this figure is important because compensation includes more than just cash distributions. It also includes benefits, auto allowance and other partner perquisites, and pension contributions.

As part of the net income analysis, firms should also compare average partner income (per the firm's financial records) with average taxable income to determine whether one firm generates a higher level of "phantom income" than the other. If the difference is significant, additional analysis to determine the cause is warranted. Firms should also exchange historical data on the timing of partner distributions (or a full cash flow schedule) as well as the relationship between the firm's net income and total partner distributions. One benefit of exchanging such data is that the firms can evaluate whether there are significant differences in the timing and magnitude of payments to equity partners.

The trend in the net income per partner average will likely raise a number of questions, including: Are the average earnings flat? Is the trend upward or downward? If upward, is it because the firm has not admitted additional partners? Is the trend up because the firm continues to lose partners and is living off inventory of departed partners? Is the trend declining because revenues are not keeping up with expense growth? These are all legitimate questions that must be answered. A decline in net income per partner does not necessarily mean partners are making less money. Adding more partners to the firm, especially by promotion of associates, may drive down the average, but have no impact on compensation levels of individual partners.

Too often, average partner compensation becomes the focal point in merger discussions. Many partners tend to assess whether they are going to be better off as a result of merger by looking only at compensation. This focus is a short-term view and does not evaluate long-term benefits of the combination. This is not to say that partner compensation is unimportant. An examination of the compensation partners can expect in the future is a critical element of a merger evaluation.

Ideally, there should be little appreciable difference in earnings for peer groups (based on performance) in the merging firms. Although each partner in a peer group may not necessarily receive equal compensation, it is important that individuals perceive they are treated fairly, given their relative contribution to the firm. Differences in compensation must be explainable. Minor compensation differences in peer groups can usually be resolved by minor adjustments for specific individuals. Typically, this approach is viewed as a short-term cost of merger and is not a problem. If, however, the differences are substantial, minor adjustments for specific individuals may not solve the problem. This problem is a potential deal breaker, but measures can be taken to overcome it. For example, the firms can allow time to move from two different compensation systems and philosophies to a single system and philosophy that is consistently applied for everyone. The transition period should be as short as possible (twelve to twenty-four months after the merger is effective).

It is critical to look beyond the numbers in this part of the analysis. It is not enough for partners to have similar earnings levels. The firms must agree on compensation philosophy. The ratio of partner compensation from high to low can lend a clue to the firm's compensation philosophy. A narrow spread may indicate that the firm has no partners who generate substantial business and can command a large percentage of net income, or the firm may not reward those partners. Lockstep compensation systems also tend to result in a narrow spread, because the points are capped at the high end and younger partners are given greater points each year, thereby diluting the percentage share for partners at the top. If one firm has a lockstep, seniority system and the other a merit-based system, it will be necessary to integrate the compensation systems or to implement a completely new system acceptable to both groups. A new compensation system or a different approach to implementation of comparable systems in the two firms might solve major differences in compensation, but it is extremely difficult to do in such a way that all partners are satisfied with the result.

Assuming that the firms are culturally and philosophically compatible, if revenue per partner and per lawyer and partner compensation levels correspond, the remaining economic questions can normally be resolved. However, even when the economics make sense, significant differences in culture and philosophy make a successful merger unlikely. (See Chapter 4.)

Expenses and Overhead per Lawyer

Expenses per lawyer include all expenses of the firm outside of partner compensation and benefits. Overhead per lawyer includes all expenses of the firm outside of the compensation and benefits paid to all timekeepers (lawyers and nonlawyers alike). Again, it is important to look closely at long-term trends as well as variances from the current budget. A highly leveraged firm (greater ratio of revenue producers to partners) will generally have a higher level of expenses on a per-lawyer basis.

In examining line-item expenses, the most important are extraordinary expenses, such as a major move or rapid expansion that might have had a significant effect on expenses in a given year. Apart from such expenses, perhaps the most valuable information from this test is a feel for the firm's standard of living and firm culture. For example, if support staff salaries are lower than normal, the firm may be concentrating more on cutting expenses than on increasing revenues.

Expenses and overhead should be analyzed by examining per-lawyer expense rather than expense or overhead ratios. These ratios are possibly the most misused and misunderstood statistics that law firms track. Many firms look at the ratios, and if they feel they are too high, they try to cut expenses. In many instances the ratios are "too high" because the firm is not producing at a sufficiently high level of gross revenue. In highly leveraged firms the margin may be high, but if profit generation also is high, cutting expenses would be counterproductive. Many firms, however, concentrate more on cutting expenses than on increasing revenue. The result is likely to be disappointing, since the biggest expense items are relatively fixed.

Leverage and Staff Ratios

The four most common ratios currently compiled in the industry include ratio of associates to partners, ratio of non-equity attorneys to equity partners, ratio of paralegals to lawyers, and ratio of administrative support staff to all legal staff. Although this last area is not critical in merger analysis, it is an important element in integrating the firms' administrative functions, and firms are monitoring ratios much more closely today. The ratios can show how well each firm is positioned to take advantage of leverage and whether enough administrative staff is available to provide the necessary support for lawyers to service clients efficiently.

Billable and Nonbillable Time

An analysis of billable and nonbillable time averages at each firm and of each timekeeper helps determine the work ethic at each firm. This is one of the most important ingredients of firm culture:

how hard are people willing to work? The hours need not match exactly, but the ranges of hours the lawyers work, or are willing to work, must be similar enough to indicate a similar lifestyle. A substantial difference in work ethic and lifestyle can be a deal breaker. In some firms, the partners may be willing to earn less to enjoy more free personal time. In other firms, billable hours might be low not because of work ethic, but because the firm's business is off. If so, billable hours are not necessarily indicative of work ethic. What is more important is whether there will be sufficient billable hours in the future.

An analysis of associate hours compared with partner hours is significant. If average associate hours are vastly different, it is necessary to determine why they are different and whether the difference signals a different culture. Average associate hours considerably lower than partner hours could indicate serious problems, such as the following:

- ◆ The partners may not delegate work. This is frequently an issue in firms with formula-based compensation systems.
- ◆ There is not enough work to keep both partners and associates busy.
- ◆ The practice management structure may be too loose, with no one responsible for ensuring that associates are busy.

Hourly Billing Rates

It is not enough to examine the standard hourly billing rates of timekeepers. It is also necessary to look at rates within peer and practice groups. Minor adjustments to individual rates are often necessary and usually present no problems.

Major disparities in billing rates can be problematic. Questions that should be asked include: Why are the rates different? Is it because of the client base? (Extremely low partner rates may indicate a high concentration of clients in a low-paying practice area.) Do low rates mean the firm is below the market? If so, the problem may be easy to resolve, provided the partners in the firm recognize it and are willing to change. If it is part of the firm's culture to keep rates lower than market as a primary competitive advantage, the firms may have different practice philosophies. A significant enough difference can spoil a possible merger.

Many firms have multiple rates for individual timekeepers. It is important to understand the specific nature of nonstandard billing rates. For example, the firm may have agreed with some clients to bill one rate for all partners and one rate for all associates. These types of arrangements often result in below-standard realization rates. This type of commitment of resources must be discussed and agreed on during the analysis.

Realization Rates

Realization is the relationship between fees collected and the value of billable hours worked (percentage of billable hours worked and valued at standard hourly rates to the actual dollars collected). The formula is as follows:

$$\begin{matrix} \text{Beginning unbilled time} \\ + \text{Beginning fee accounts} \\ \text{receivable} + \text{Value of} \\ \text{billable time worked} \end{matrix} - \begin{matrix} \text{Ending unbilled} \\ \text{time} + \text{Ending} \\ \text{fee accounts} \\ \text{receivable} \end{matrix} = \begin{matrix} \text{Potential} \\ \text{fees} \\ \text{to be} \\ \text{collected} \end{matrix}$$

$$\text{Realization} = \frac{\text{Fees collected}}{\text{Potential fees to be collected}}$$

Use of the accrual concept of inventory neutralizes timing differences. This formula can be modified to calculate billing realization separate from collection realization.

Realization rates say a good deal about a firm. For example, a firm with an overall realization rate above 95 percent of standard rates is probably doing an excellent job of billing and collecting accounts or doing a good deal of premium billing. Realization rates consistently below 90 percent may indicate a number of unprofitable practice areas, inadequate work intake procedures, partners doing associate work and having to write off the time, inadequate billing and collection guidelines, or inadequate partner accountability. Billing practices are very much a part of firm culture and philosophy. Wide differences in overall realization (or even billing or collection realization alone) could be a problem and must be reconciled.

Work in Progress, Accounts Receivable, and Inventory Turnover

Work in progress per lawyer and accounts receivable per lawyer are key statistics, especially in terms of projecting cash flow for the merged firm. Billing and collection habits, average amounts per lawyer, aging, and turnover all tell a lot about an individual firm's cash flow management and potential cash flow issues for the merged firm.

Inventory turnover, for purposes of this analysis, is defined as the average number of months of revenue collected, represented by the amount of work in progress and accounts receivable. This calculation is crucial for cash flow planning. This computation gives, on average, the amount of time it takes the firm to convert a billable hour worked into cash.

$$\text{Turnover} = \frac{\text{Work in progress} + \text{Accounts receivable}}{\text{Average monthly value of billable time worked}}$$

An evaluation of the aging of work in progress and accounts receivable is important for many reasons. First, aging can help the firms make value judgments regarding ultimate collectibility. (Before any merger takes place, it is a good idea to evaluate all old unbilled matters and receivables to determine collectibility and to facilitate planning for the merged firm.) Second, old work may highlight areas that warrant further discussion. For example, a high percentage of old unbilled time may indicate contingency work, a special billing arrangement, or simply a failure to write off bad accounts. A high level of old accounts receivable may represent bankruptcy work, estate administration, litigation, a client unable to pay, or a problem with the services performed. High accumulations of time in either work in progress or accounts receivable can indicate a loose practice management structure under which partners are allowed considerable autonomy in billing and collecting receivables. This problem must be resolved before culmination of the merger.

Collections from Top Clients

There is no magic number of clients that should be analyzed in evaluating collections from top clients. Depending on firm size, the number analyzed is typically anywhere from twenty to fifty. The client dependency test, which consists of looking at the percentage of fees received from top clients during a three-year period, is important for several purposes:

- To assess the stability of the client base. Are the same clients top clients year after year, or is the practice transactional? In a transactional practice, a large portion of the firm's business must be replaced each year. If so, it may be necessary to look at fees for years when a particular client is not in the top group.
- To define the extent to which the firm relies on any one client or a small group of clients (e.g., top five, top ten, and top twenty). For example, if one firm depends heavily on one client for a substantial amount of its income, the other firm must satisfy itself that the client will stay with the merged firm. This data is also analyzed to determine *major* client conflicts.
- To identify each firm's dependence on a particular industry group for a certain percentage of annual fees.
- To quantify each firm's reliance on referrals from other firms. Many small, specialized firms rely on law firm referrals. Merging such a firm with a full-service firm may result in a loss of referral work.

Although it is important to look at top fee-producing clients, the top clients may not account for a large percentage of the firm's total collections. Therefore, it is necessary to look beyond the top clients to understand more fully the nature of the firm's client base, including types of client, types of work, and fees commanded for that work. Client dependency figures can help gauge the firm's ability to attract and replace business and to generate additional business from existing clients.

Capitalization

Law firms must continually confront the means by which day-to-day business will be funded. Various funding mechanisms include partner contribution to capital, low partner draws in relation to expected compensation (e.g., 60 percent of compensation), and borrowing. It is difficult to make general statements about adequate levels of capitalization without knowing the law firm. However, law firms need adequate funds to manage the business and to provide for growth. To determine each firm's fiscal philosophy, it is important to understand each firm's method of capitalization and the extent to which partners have contributed actual dollars. Have partners bought into their share of work in progress or accounts receivable? What is the basis for capital contributions? How is the needed level of capital determined? When do partners buy in, and how?

Valuation of Assets

If either firm contributes fixed assets to the merged entity, the basis of valuation must be discussed and agreed on. The value of fixed assets is most often determined on the basis of book value, as calculated for tax purposes to eliminate any differences associated with the firm's depreciation policies used for internal reporting. Valuation of inventory (work in progress, accounts receivable) is more complex, often involving in-depth review of each component of inventory. The purpose of valuing assets is to be sure that, on a per-partner basis, both firms are contributing approximately the same value to the combined firm. The value being contributed, assuming a pooling of assets, forms the basis for credit in an individual partner's capital account. Since it is unlikely that the capital credited will be exactly the amount required for the merging firm, it is not unusual to agree that any excess capital balance will be paid out over time or any deficient balance will be paid in over time.

Some firms lease equipment. Each firm should fully understand the extent of such ongoing obligations. Some firms own or have equity positions in their buildings. These situations also must be considered in the financial analysis. For example, if the partners own the building, how is rent determined? If the firms merge, will all partners receive the opportunity to become owners? If so, on what basis?

Liabilities

It is important to examine the nature of all liabilities and potential liabilities, including any assertion of malpractice claims, unfunded obligations, and other off-balance-sheet liabilities. This would also include an analysis of the firms' operating leases.

There are two basic levels of external financing. The first level of financing is to acquire external debt to purchase fixed assets. This level of financing is typically done with long-term debt amortized over a period of years equal to the depreciable life of the asset. The second level is line of credit debt used to help finance cash flow. As part of the merger analysis, the firms should exchange details of each firm's loan repayment schedule as well as a summary of the reasons why the debt was incurred in the first place.

Clearly, each firm's philosophy of incurring debt must be discussed fully. Debt philosophy should be examined in conjunction with a capitalization plan and the compensation system. For example, does the firm regularly use a line of credit for short-term operating needs? Does the firm borrow to pay partners? Does the firm borrow to fund expansion? Will the firm borrow for capital expenditures, or does it lease furniture and equipment? What level of borrowing is the firm willing to accept? Are partners expected to contribute minimum amounts of capital before the firm will borrow money? It is critical that the firms reach agreement on these issues.

Investment of additional funds may be necessary to make the merged entity operate smoothly. This investment can come from three sources: additional capital contributions, current earnings, and loans. The decision often hinges on whether the partners are willing to earn less or incur the additional risks.

In discussing current debt, the firms must determine whether one is willing to assume the debt of the second firm and vice versa. The less willing the partners are to pool all assets and liabilities, the less likely it is the two firms will integrate.

Retirement, Withdrawal, Disability, and Death Benefits

Most firm agreements describe in some detail the firm's obligations to departing lawyers. These obligations cover events such as death, disability, retirement, expulsion, and withdrawal. The firms must examine benefits currently payable and future exposure because these liabilities can affect future income. Firms that have limited or no unfunded benefits because they established funding mechanisms are much better off than firms that must rely on future earnings to fund these obligations.

To the extent that any of these benefits are unfunded, a present value must be calculated to assess the impact on the combined firm. In addition, a projection must be made to show how funding these obligations will affect the combined firm. Each of these obligations should be reviewed in the context of the benefit plans and the compensation philosophy. Capitalization also may be affected, depending on how shares or interests are valued. The period of payment also must be considered.

Compensation of Income/ Non-Equity Partners and Associates

Compensation of income partners and associates is rarely a deal breaker, but both types of compensation should be discussed in the context of what it will cost to merge (i.e., cost to eliminate any wide differences in compensation between comparably performing individuals) and what policies and procedures are used to promote individuals. An analysis of income partner and associate compensation typically entails preparing a chart for each firm showing earnings by bar admission date and productivity statistics over a multiyear period. If there are significant differences in compensation relative to apparent contribution to the firm, it is necessary to determine the cause.

Developing the Pro Forma Projections

6

Introduction

The economic evaluation does not end with the historical financial analysis. The historical analysis is a necessary step taken early in the process to help gauge initial economic compatibility. It will help each firm develop greater comfort about going forward in assessing cultural and philosophical compatibility and resolving other key issues.

Assuming the historical financial performance tests are encouraging, pro forma financial projections need to be developed to estimate the expected financial performance of the merged entity for the two to three years after the merger effective date. To make projections beyond the first year, it is necessary to develop assumptions regarding how quickly the merged firm will integrate the practices and benefit from the expected merger synergy.

Development of a pro forma depends on reasonable assumptions agreed to by the merger committee. (See Exhibit 16 on page 153 for a checklist of items usually discussed at a meeting to begin work on pro forma projections.) The firms can select assumptions that are aggressive or conservative. At times, firms may consider developing multiple pro formas based on differing assumptions. This can be a useful exercise; however, only one version should be presented to partners in a merger vote. The development of the pro formas *must* be done in consideration of the business case for the merger and strategic goals of the new entity. It cannot be treated as a simple, mechanical exercise.

The best the merged firm can hope for during the first year is that partners will maintain their current level of net income per partner. The benefits of the merger are more likely to be realized in the longer term (most likely after a minimum of eighteen to twenty-four months).

Pro Forma Income Statement

Exhibit 17 on pages 156–158 is an example of a pro forma income statement projection typically used in merger analysis. The preparation of the pro forma involves much more than simply adding the two firms' income statements plus a percentage growth rate for revenue and expenses. While the basis of the pro forma is each firm's latest projection of its stand-alone results for the current year (or next year's budget), an effective pro forma goes far beyond a simple income statement consolidation.

For starters, the two firms have to compare their stand-alone budgets and understand the basis for making certain assumptions. This step will give each firm clues as to how the other firm plans and forecasts performance for the coming year. To increase each firm's comfort with the projections, each should look at prior-year projections compared with actual performance.

Revenue Projection

The merger's effect on revenue during the first year is difficult to predict. While the firm may experience some synergistic growth, it may also experience a reduction in revenue due to the nonbillable time commitment related to integrating the two firms. Often, a conservative revenue assumption is to project no net change or a reduction in the sum of the two projected stand-alone revenues. Because most merged firms want to be conservative with their projections, it is rare to see a merger where the combined revenue is adjusted upward significantly.

To develop the revenue projection, firms typically start with their current budget (or, better yet, latest reprojection of the budget) and then make adjustments for the following expected changes:

- ◆ *Expected change in billable hours, billing rates, or realization after the merger.* Some of these adjustments may be the direct result of the historical financial analysis. For example, if the historical analysis indicates that one firm's rates are well below market, the firms may decide to build into the pro forma some portion of the rate differential as the firm tries to increase its rates to market levels.

- ◆ *Expected change in the number of lawyers after the merger.* Here, the firms need to consider and adjust for the potential loss of lawyers who decide that they do not want to be part of the merged firm (and for the associated loss of revenue). The firms also need to add projections for new hires who join the firm after the effective date of the combination (and for their associated revenue).

The revenue projection needs to be made for each year of the pro forma period. A word of caution: It is extremely important that the pro forma not overestimate the merger firm's revenue and, more importantly, overall profits. Overpromising in the pro forma and then failing to deliver can result in significant, long-term negative feelings toward the merger itself and toward those who helped draft the pro forma.

Expense Adjustments

The firms also need to develop multiyear expense projections. While there may be some duplication of costs that can be eliminated, it is almost always necessary to project additional costs in the pro forma. The typical expense adjustments and approaches that can be used to make these projections are discussed below. These adjustments are often separated into two categories: one-time merger costs and ongoing operating expenses. This separation allows the pro forma statement to show the short-term impact of the merger (potential revenue loss, certain one-time costs) and provides an estimate of ongoing merger operations after the merger. It is critical here to have the detailed budget assumptions available. To estimate the magnitude of the adjustments, it is necessary to know the details of the original projections. The following items are those that may require adjustments.

Associate Salaries

Firms need to compare the current wages and bonuses payable to the associates (as well as non-equity timekeepers). It is not unusual to find that the salary scales of the two firms differ, depending on their locations. If the two firms are located in the same city, adjustments are usually made at the effective date of the merger to reflect the higher of the two salary scales. This cost is an additional one that the firms must recognize.

Likewise, the bonus systems for associates must be examined to determine if any adjustments are needed. While geographic differences may justify salary differences, the firm's policy regarding bonuses must be evaluated. There may be some justification for paying associate bonuses in one location and not another, but this would be rare.

Other Salaries

The salaries and bonuses for administrative staff must be analyzed and projected. In most instances, there is a potential cost savings to be realized, particularly with support staff. The merged firm will not, for example, need two accounting departments. However, during the assimilation period, a great deal of administrative integration will be necessary to bring the two systems together. Although the merged firm will have duplicate positions, they may be necessary to get all the work done.

Benefits

Part of the examination of administrative issues is an analysis of benefits provided to partners and employees. Employers usually provide health, life, disability, and other insurance, as well as contributory or noncontributory retirement plans. Given most employees' concern about changes in their employee benefits, the group or committee assigned the task of aligning the firms' benefit plans is in an unenviable position. Ultimately, certain employees will welcome a change in benefits, while others will dread any adjustment. Therefore, it is important that employees receive in a timely manner accurate information regarding potential changes.

Although it is not essential to resolve benefits issues before the merger, the level of coverage each firm provides must be analyzed to determine whether they differ. Depending on the complexities of the various plans and the differences between them, each firm may keep its own benefits for one year and, after investigating alternatives, develop a single benefits package. In mergers of smaller firms, it is common for the employees of one firm to be brought into the benefits package of the larger firm. The pro forma should reflect any incremental costs or savings resulting from the combination.

One situation that requires caution is the merger of a partnership with a professional corporation. There are some special circumstances to consider, including payroll taxes for shareholders (there are no payroll taxes for partners) and insurance benefits for shareholders shown on an income statement (not so for partners).

Occupancy Costs

There must be a clear understanding of the terms of each firm's office lease, including lease terms, cost per square foot, pass-throughs for building costs and taxes, expansion options, amount of available space, utilities, storage, parking, and the like. When the merging firms have offices in the same cities, the firms must determine whether the merged firm can be consolidated into one space or will continue to carry two office leases. If offices are consolidated, will the merged firm need to write off the value of certain leasehold improvements? In some situations, assumptions will be made for subleasing excess space.

Some costs are often overlooked. In a multicity merger it is often desirable to have lawyers move between offices temporarily or to relocate permanently. A cost estimate for moving must be included in the pro forma. Another cost that is often overlooked is leasehold improvements to house the new lawyers. Although these improvements are treated as a capital cost, the effect of the additional cost (depreciation and any interest on loans) must be considered.

Office Supplies and Expenses

A merger requires new letterhead, stationery, business cards, marketing materials, and the like. These are typically one-time costs that must be absorbed as a result of the merger. In the long term, this area and others that rely on outside vendors may provide some economies of scale resulting from increased buying power for the larger law firm.

Technology and Communications

Integrating the technology of the two firms, including conversion and training, adds costs. A major issue for the merged firm is how to share and disseminate information. The challenge is how to make the multitude of technologies compatible (be they e-mail, document management, calendaring, financial, etc.). This effort must consider integrating telephone systems and voice and data communications and providing services for these systems, including the capacity of the telephone system. A merger of firms in different cities usually requires installation of dedicated lines to link the offices.

The cost of internal communication is often overlooked. Not only do firms have to consider this cost, but it also serves as a reminder that increased internal communications will be key to the merger's success.

For mergers of firms in different locations, circulating documents among offices is another cost. Cost of messenger services, overnight delivery, or other means of transmittal should be projected. A firm intranet is helpful for circulating documents and information among offices.

Malpractice Insurance

Firms must share the details of their insurance policies, including coverage, excess limits, deductible, claims history, and outstanding claims. At the effective date of the merger, the lawyers must all be covered under one policy. Depending on the nature of each firm's coverage, a tail policy may be required to cover acts before the merger.

Firms may be able to realize cost savings in this area. Some policies permit adding lawyers during the year at no additional premium. In some instances the merged firm may realize a lower cost per lawyer, depending on the carrier.

Firm Meetings

The category of firm meetings includes provision for additional travel costs related to integrating the practices and administration. A goal of the merger should be to get the lawyers and staff acting as though they are part of one firm. This goal will take a great deal of time and effort. Mergers of firms in different cities or states can be particularly costly because of out-of-pocket costs as well as the time commitment.

There are also costs for managing the firm and the practice groups. In the early months, significant time should be spent managing the new entity. The time and cost involved in transporting lawyers and administrative personnel during the critical assimilation and integration period can be significant. Newly merged firms can benefit from practice group retreats and firmwide retreats. The practice group can use retreats to develop departmental goals and business plans. The firmwide retreat is an opportunity to get all the partners (or lawyers) together to meet each other in a social atmosphere, plan, and set the course for the firm for the coming years.

Business Development

The costs of business development should not be overlooked. Merger is primarily for business development and marketing reasons. However, many firms ignore the adage "You have to spend money to make money." Sufficient funds must be allocated to achieve the goals for merger. That means devoting the necessary time and dollars.

During the first year of the merger, the merged firm must be willing to spend additional funds on business development efforts with existing clients, prospects, and other key decision makers. These efforts include meetings to advise the groups of the additional services and capabilities available and to introduce them to the new partners.

The firm brochure, Web site, and other institutional marketing materials must be updated following a merger. The firm must decide how much it is willing to spend on such efforts. A one-time cost of the merger is for announcements, client mailings, and receptions for client development. The cost for these items depends on how much the partners are willing (or need) to spend.

Fixed-Asset-Related Expenses

Expenses associated with fixed assets include costs related to equipment leases, maintenance and repairs, depreciation and amortization, and interest expense. The adjustments to the budget are based on the combined firm's needs to integrate technology, purchase additional furniture and equipment, improve or renovate space, and recognize interest for borrowings that may be necessary to fund cash flow (considering the one-time costs related to the merger).

Outside Professional Services

It is common for the merging firms to incur costs for outside professional services. Examples are consulting services for key merger issues, financial analysis of the two firms, preparation of the pro forma, tax advice, legal and technical advice on pension and retirement plans, technical advice on the integration of technology, and advice on the integration process. All of these costs need to be built into the pro forma.

Summary

Once these expense adjustments have been added to the stand-alone budgets, the merger committee can review the merged firm's projection for the first twelve months' operation. The next step is to project the firm's expenses for years two and three of the pro forma period. The projection for the first year serves as the base for the following years' projection, with appropriate adjustments to eliminate one-time merger costs and add new costs (e.g., added expenses due to growth and planned occupancy changes) related to the merger firm's operations.

Partners must be aware of the short-term economic impact of the merger. It is critical that the partners be reminded that merger is not a short-term proposition. The pro formas are presented to prevent any misunderstanding that there will likely be a short-term cost and a long-term benefit.

Pro Forma Cash Flow Projection

In addition to a pro forma income statement, it is necessary to prepare a pro forma cash flow statement. This statement will show the merger's impact on the cash position of each firm, which may affect the cash available for distribution to the partners. Exhibit 18 (page 159) is a sample cash flow statement. The approach used for the income statement can be used for the cash flow projection. The following list illustrates the types of adjustments that may be required to arrive at available cash:

- ◆ *Depreciation and amortization.* The adjustment for the cash flow should be identical to the adjustment made in the pro forma income statement. Remember also that any leasehold improvement write-offs are expenses for tax purposes but have no impact on cash flow. These items do not reduce cash and therefore must be added back to net income.
- ◆ *Purchases of fixed assets.* Adjustments must be made to cash for anticipated expenditures for the acquisition of fixed assets that have not already been expensed on the income statement. Fixed asset acquisitions may have already been expensed on the income statement, as in the case of books and minor equipment purchases (e.g., cal-

culators, lamps, portable dictating machines). Items should not be included here if already included elsewhere. However, this adjustment should include any purchases of assets, regardless of the source of funds.

♦ *Proceeds from bank borrowing.* An adjustment should be made for any anticipated bank loan resulting from the merger. This should not be a net amount. Whether the firm borrows from a line of credit or enters into a term note, the total amount should appear on this line.

♦ *Repayment of bank debt.* An adjustment for any changes to anticipated repayment schedules shown in the stand-alone budgets should be included.

♦ *Partner contributions of capital.* Any additional paid-in cash that has not already been provided for in the stand-alone projections is included here. It is unusual to see additional paid-in cash as an adjustment in the pro forma. It can occur, however, when the firms agree to merge the two capital plans and require the partners immediately to provide funds equal to the required level.

♦ *Partner withdrawals of permanent capital.* It is not unusual to have partners leave as a result of a merger. Depending on the agreements, the firm may have an obligation to return capital (cash).

The preparation of a cash flow projection is an important ingredient in the merger process. Although frequently ignored, it is an important consideration when contemplating capital acquisitions and in resolving issues of partner compensation, including establishing a method of draws.

The Economic Balance Sheet

7

Introduction

In the United States, the vast majority of law firms utilize a modified cash basis method of accounting. With this method, fees receivable and unbilled time are not recorded as revenue until collected. Similarly, contingent liabilities such as unfunded retirement obligations and certain other firm obligations are not recorded. While a discussion of the pros and cons of the modified cash system are outside the scope of this book, it is clear that the system does not provide sufficient balance sheet information for merging two law firms, each with significant unrecorded assets and liabilities. To provide a more accurate picture of the true economic value that each firm brings to the table, it is much more useful to capture off-balance-sheet items and ensure consistency of approach on the balance sheet. Without the big picture of how all these factors work together, firms tend to emphasize differences in one component of the balance sheet (for example, debt) without understanding the factors that might balance that one component.

An economic balance sheet (EBS), such as the example in Exhibit 19 on pages 160–161, expands the cash-basis balance sheet by quantifying the relative economic position of each firm and comparing the on- and off-balance-sheet assets and liabilities that each constituent firm contributes to the merged firm. Most often, the adjustments include the addition of assets equal to the projected realizable value of fee inventory (work in progress and accounts receivable), the elimination of undistributed earnings that will be paid out to equity partners in short order, and the addition of liabilities for the present value of unfunded retirement plans, other commitments to retired and retiring partners, significant differences in lease obligations, outstanding claims against the firm, and at times, significant differences in deferred expenses/payables. Clearly, it is important to have realistic valuations of each asset and liability. On the EBS, each firm's "economic capital" represents assets less liabilities less paid-in capital and other capital amounts including undistributed income.

The EBS should not be viewed as a basic mechanical, accounting exercise. Instead, it should be viewed as a critical component of the merger financial analysis, which requires a rigorous assessment of on- and off-balance-sheet assets and liabilities. The primary goal is to determine whether or not the net value that each firm is contributing to the new firm is consistent with that of the other firm, based on per-partner averages, relative share of profits, and relative share of contributed capital.

EBS Date

Merging firms typically prepare a draft EBS well before the merger effective date in order to spot any glaring balance sheet inconsistencies. Most often, the firms will prepare this draft using data dated as of the prior year-end or sometimes as of the date one year before the anticipated effective date. The reason firms choose these dates is that they typically serve as the best proxy for what the firms' asset and liability positions will be as of the effective date. Of course, the actual results will undoubtedly be different as of the effective date. Consequently, it is important that a final EBS be done as of the effective date.

Once the final numbers have been agreed upon by the new firm's management committee, the value of each legacy firm's contribution of economic capital to the new firm will be fixed, and any required balancing adjustments will be made.

Asset Assessment

One of the trickiest and sometimes most contentious aspects of the EBS is the valuation of fee inventory. When calculating the realizable value, it is important to use a consistent valuation method for each firm. Often, it is helpful to have an objective outsider perform the analysis, since it requires asking difficult questions about the collectibility of inventory.

Most often, inventory is valued one of three ways: by applying one realization rate to all inventory (using historical averages), by applying separate realization rates to inventory based on specific inventory aging categories, or by performing a detailed analysis of each inventory item and applying individual realization rates to each. In practice, the most common method is to apply separate rates to each aging category. Frequently, firms follow this method but delete certain matters that are absolutely known to be unrecoverable or need to be separately valued outside an aging analysis (e.g., contingent matters that may have a high realizable value but where work in progress is very old because the matter has not been billed).

A number of noninventory items also may affect the ultimate outcome of the EBS and require discussion or significant analysis. Examples include the following balance sheet issues:

- ◆ Are the firms using consistent depreciation methods?
- ◆ Should the appreciated/market value of one firm's artwork or other unique assets be included?
- ◆ What impact will technology integration have on the useful life of both firms' equipment and software? Do some of

the fixed assets on the balance sheet actually have no value following the merger?

EBS Analysis

As with the financial profile, it is helpful to prepare the EBS in a side-by-side format that allows for quick comparison of the firms' results. While the bottom-line, gross results of the EBS are important, firms also need to look at the relative, per-equity-partner value of the individual components. It is also important, particularly for firms whose income per partner may differ, to look at the relative balances overall. Ideally, the percentage of one firm's capital compared with the sum of both firms' capital should be similar to the percentage of that firm's net income compared with combined income. But as in any analysis, there is no one number that tells the whole story, so it is important to look at the whole picture and really understand factors behind the numbers as well.

In addition to basic comparison tests such as assets per equity partner and liabilities per equity partner, it is useful to compare the following measures:

- *Contributed capital.* This should be analyzed both on a per-partner basis and relative to profit allocation. Significant differences in contributed capital per partner may indicate potentially troublesome cultural differences regarding the willingness of partners to make a cash investment in their firm. The comparison of contributed capital versus profit allocation is useful to assess each firm's expected "return" (in terms of compensation), given the firm's total capital contributed.

- *Debt load.* Here, comparisons are commonly made between debt load and net fixed assets and between debt load and contributed capital. At a minimum, the comparison of debt load to fixed assets can reveal whether a firm is borrowing to fund operations (if debt exceeds fixed assets), including partner compensation. The comparison of

debt load to contributed capital can identify whether partners are willing to contribute capital to the firm or prefer
to have the bank finance the firm's operations.

◆ *Unfunded obligations to retiring or former partners.* Fortu-
nately, many firms have taken steps to limit their exposure
to unfunded obligations. In firms that still have unfunded
obligations, it is important to include the present value of
the obligations on the EBS, since the present value can significantly affect the relative economic contribution of the
two firms. Including the present value can also help the firm
that is not bringing the obligation to the deal get a better
feel for the level of obligation it may be taking on. At times,
seeing the magnitude of the liability can help the firm with
the obligation understand that something needs to be done
to limit the firm's exposure, regardless of merger.

Equalizing the EBS and Resolving Issues

Once the EBS has been prepared, the firms may need to look for opportunities to balance out any significant differences. In most cases,
expect to see some difference in average per-partner economic capital and in some cases these differences will be material. Perhaps
the best way to evaluate capital is on a per-compensation-point
basis, if compensation has been resolved and integrated before the
merger. The threshold question is at what point some level of equalization is needed. In some mergers per-partner differences of
$50,000 or more go unadjusted. In others equalizing adjustments
are made for differences well below $50,000. When adjustments are
made, they can include the following:

◆ A capital credit may be allocated to one firm, usually the
smaller firm, to reflect the economic value that the firm is
bringing beyond its paid-in capital. Normally this happens
when the smaller firm's paid-in capital is significantly
lower than the larger firm's position and is in lieu of asking
the partners to come up with additional capital on the

merger date. However, some firms are wary of giving capital credits like this, because it can be viewed as unfair by the partners of the larger firm.

♦ Assets may be left out of the transaction to lower one firm's economic value to a more comparable level (e.g., a particular continguency matter or other accounts receivable).

♦ Certain assets may be dedicated to certain liabilities. For example, a firm may choose to hold out of the deal inventory that has been of very little value and to use the collections from that inventory, if any, to offset a liability that is not being brought into the merger (e.g., an unfunded retirement plan).

♦ Unfunded obligations may be reduced. Firms tend to focus more on reducing or eliminating unfunded obligations when they see that liability as a major stumbling block for an otherwise beneficial merger.

♦ Additional capital may be contributed or excess paid out. In some instances, the primary discrepancy on the EBS is a difference in contributed capital between the two firms. Before deciding how to deal with the imbalance in capital accounts, it is important to determine the capital policy for the new firm. For example, while returning excess capital to partners in one firm may make sense, it may not be logical to do that if the combined firm's capital policy will just require all partners to add capital to the new firm anyway. Thus, the resolution of the capital imbalance is intertwined with the decision on the capital policy for the new firm.

♦ The excess value contributed by one firm may be paid off. One method of equalization is through actual cash payments from one partner group to the other. If large, the payments are often spread over several years. Most often, the firms isolate certain accounts receivable and work in progress as of the effective date of the merger and allocate the cash collected from this inventory to the partners of the firm with excess economic capital. Over time, the excess capital payments to the one group of partners help re-equalize economic capital throughout the combined firm.

It is rare for the side-by-side EBS to line up perfectly between the constituent firms. More often, the EBS identifies equalization needed to adjust the interests in the contributed assets, both net cash basis and net accrual basis, of the two groups of partners in the ongoing firm. If the firms identify the drivers of the differences and then reach a compromise regarding their resolution, the EBS can usually be completed and serve as one more tool that supports the law firm merger. However, it is important in a merger discussion that the partners not lose sight of the ultimate objective, which is to do a merger that makes the combined firm more competitive in the marketplace. The advantages on the income side should more than make up for minor differences on the balance sheet side if the merger is a good one.

Getting to a Decision 8

Introduction

There is no easy way or step-by-step checklist to help a firm decide whether a proposed merger makes sense. The evaluation process is time-consuming, and it cannot and should not be hurried. At the same time, the process should move at a pace that maintains a certain level of excitement and momentum.

The decision to merge is not one decision. Rather, it is a series of decisions that have been made at each step of the evaluation process. For the firms to proceed to the next set of decisions, tentative consensus must have been reached on previous issues. As each issue is discussed, evaluated, and resolved, the level of comfort between the two groups increases, and enthusiasm builds. As the process unfolds and the two groups work together to resolve the issues through compromise, trust begins to build, and each group can begin to see the relative pros and cons of the prospective merger. It should become clear to the partners that the benefits sufficiently outweigh any disadvantages to approving the merger.

Each group can also begin to see what it is going to take to sell the merger to their partners.

It is also important to build into the merger discussions several stopping points where each firm can step back and reach a go–no go conclusion. While speed and enthusiasm are important, it is also important not to get caught up in the excitement of getting the deal done. It is also useful for both firms to have confirmation that the other firm remains committed to the deal.

Once the major issues have been discussed and resolved, it is time to give the partners the information they need to make a decision about whether to merge.

How to Get Information to the Partners

There are a number of ways to get information to the partners. The delicate balance that must be struck is the timing of communication and the distribution of written materials. On the one hand, the merger committee does not want to be accused of withholding information from partners; on the other, committee members don't want to distribute materials that are incomplete or inaccurate. This is particularly true with financial information about the merged firm. To avoid creating inappropriate expectations, financial information should be distributed only when it is final.

Throughout the evaluation process, meetings keep partners informed, provide an opportunity for the lawyers in the two firms to get to know each other, and begin to build consensus on the various issues that must be addressed. Most firms schedule social events between the two groups as well. (See Chapter 4.)

During the process of addressing and resolving various merger issues, partners are often called on to give their views on certain topics under discussion. Such partner discussions are vital to the merger committee for testing the waters, obtaining feedback and giving direction on whether the planned course of action should be modified and further steps that should be taken, and building consensus for the ultimate decision to merge.

Except in small firms, there are too many issues to resolve to take each issue to the partners for approval. Therefore, a merger committee becomes the spokesperson for the firm. The merger committee then gives the partners periodic updates on the status of the discussions and estimated timetables for completion. The extent of partner involvement in larger firms depends on the firm's culture. A democratic firm will find it necessary to build consensus throughout the process (although this should be true for all firms). The challenge is to recognize which issues should be partnership ones and which issues should be driven by the firm's leadership. The danger of taking too many issues to the full partnership is that the vocal minority may significantly influence the discussions. Negotiations will then take place on two levels: within each firm and between the two firms.

The merger committee should have the authority to carry out its mission. It is the committee's responsibility to determine if the merger makes sense and, if so, to recommend approval to the partners. The committee's responsibility also includes providing partners with information they need to make their final decision on the merger. Although the partners will vote the merger up or down, partner reactions and decisions can be affected by associate and staff feelings about the proposed merger. Nonpartners also should receive relevant information on a periodic, appropriate basis.

The Merger Notebook or Prospectus

Getting the information compiled and presented in a format that is readable and easy to understand is key to getting to a vote in a businesslike manner. Many large firms have used a merger notebook (sometimes loosely referred to as a prospectus) to compile and disseminate the relevant merger information.

These prospectuses can range from a full set of information to a written summary that presents the key facts. This often depends on firm culture and expectations of the partners. A shorter written document (e.g., twenty pages) is more likely to be read by a greater percentage of the partners. Exhibit 20 on pages 162–163 shows a sample table of contents. The major components might include the following:

- Profiles of each of the firms, including firm history, lawyers, practice specialties, key clients, and the like.
- A discussion of acknowledged practice synergy and possible strategic plans.
- Terms of the merger, including a detailed summary of the proposed resolution of key issues, including firm name, governance, capital, and voting.
- Client conflicts analysis.
- Practice group report summaries.
- Business development and marketing opportunities.
- Detailed comparative financial profile and analysis and pro forma financial projections for at least the first year of the combined firm.

Some firms distribute the merger notebook/prospectus to all partners. Others, for confidentiality reasons, choose to make the notebook available for review but do not distribute it widely. Others choose a combination, distributing a short prospectus but making the detailed information available to partners who want more information.

It is also important for the material distributed to be essentially the same at both firms. While there may be some information that is relevant only to one or the other, consistency in the analysis, interpretation, and business case is important, since if the merger is successful, the partners of each firm will be each other's partners.

In mergers involving small and midsize firms, it may not be practical to compile a comprehensive merger notebook. In these situations, the majority of the partners are much more involved in the process and have received the information over the time of the discussions. However, the fact that partners are more involved in the process does not eliminate the need to compile the basic information in one complete package for distribution to partners. Much of this information is needed for partners to make an intelligent decision on the merits of the merger. Minimum requirements are a comparative financial report, pro forma financial projections, and a "term" sheet. The term sheet includes a brief description of key items, such as effective date of merger, method of combination, firm management, partner compensation, partner capital, and the way the combined firm proposes to operate. In the case of some small-firm mergers, partners have found that they can skip this step by going directly to drafting a letter of intent.

After distributing the relevant merger information, it is beneficial to schedule one or more informational meetings with the partners to further present the business case and answer any questions they have. These meetings are typically scheduled within a week of distribution of materials. These meetings provide an opportunity for the partners to get clarification on any items presented in the material and to raise any questions or concerns on issues related to the merger. The session should not be allowed to degenerate into a reopening of each merger-related issue. Commonly, partners view this as an opportunity to hear the merger committee endorse the merger firsthand and to hear the reasons why the committee favors the merger. Although there may have been a great deal of research, analysis, and discussion, the partners will ultimately have to rely on their instincts and the firm leadership's assurance that this merger is in the best long-term interest of the firm and the partners.

Scheduling a Vote

Each firm must meet the voting requirements contained in its firm agreement. The vote at both firms should be scheduled for the same day if possible, although some firms have scheduled them on back-to-back days. If the evaluation process has followed the systematic approach outlined in this book and the informational sessions have been used to address any final concerns the partners may have, the actual vote becomes a mere formality.

The recommendation on the merger should not go to the partners, however, until the merger committee and the firm's management group are certain that the vote for a merger is assured. A close vote or the need to debate the issue can be extremely divisive. Usually, it means that the merger committee and the firm's management group have gotten too far afield from their partners, have not been sensitive enough to partners' views, or may not have involved the partners enough in the process.

Merger Agreement

Once the vote has been taken and the merger approved, the real work begins. Chapter 9 deals with how to integrate the two firms, which will determine the ultimate success of the combined firms.

The firms may want to consult with outside counsel to determine the best way to document the merger and the decisions made. For example, it is not unusual to see the two partnerships amend their own partnership agreements to reflect the merger and the decisions that have been made. It may, though, be as simple as making reference to a package of materials that will govern the firm between the time the merger is approved and the merger's effective date (or later if the merged firm's partnership agreement is not ready to be signed).

Legal documents must be prepared to acknowledge the fact that the required number of partners of the two firms have approved the merger. This documentation can take a number of different forms, and there is no right or wrong approach. In fact, these merger-related agreements have a number of different names but accomplish the same things. The document may be as simple as a letter of intent signed by both firms or as formal as a merger agreement.

A typical merger agreement covers the major aspects of the merger (see Exhibit 21 on pages 164–167), including:

- ◆ Name of the combined firm.
- ◆ Effective date of the merger.
- ◆ Method of combination.

- Governance structure, including decisions reserved to partners, voting, and day-to-day management.
- Compensation system, including a transitional approach, if one is necessary.
- Deferred compensation benefits, including those for voluntary withdrawal, expulsion, death, disability, and retirement.
- Capital structure, including the capital position desired for the firm and the way individual partners' capital requirements will be determined and paid.
- Practice management structure.
- Any other major issues resolved in the merger discussions.

Deciding to merge is difficult and sometimes emotional, even though a long series of events has brought the firm to the final vote. The key to getting to a decision is to make decisions all along the way, based on a long-term outlook. If a timetable and action plan are not charted out and responsibilities are not designated at the beginning, the merger may very easily die of its own weight. The decision to merge should be based on the strength of the business case but ultimately will be based on each partner's sense of whether he or she will be better off in the merged firm. Therefore, seeing that the partners get all the information they need to make an educated decision is very important. A willingness to compromise also may help to bring the partners to a decision, as well as ease post-merger integration. (See the next chapter.)

Integrating the Firms 9

Introduction

Merger integration can, and should, begin as soon as the decision to merge is made. At that point, both firms must move immediately to integrate practice management and administrative systems. (See Chapter 10.) The more work that can be done before the firms actually merge, the better, regardless of the type of merger.

Integrating immediately incurs costs outside those of the merger analysis. These costs include the following:

- Public relations and communications to the press, clients, and other contacts.
- Physical integration of any offices.
- Development of an overall administrative plan.
- Practice group meetings.
- Joint visits to clients and prospective clients.

Usually, the firms will agree to share costs. Depending on circumstances, such as relative size of the firms or the nature of the expenditures, the firms may share costs equally, pro rata based on the number of lawyers, or on some other agreed-on basis. Once the decision to merge has been made, the firms should be willing to spend money to integrate immediately. The benefits of early integration far outweigh the costs.

In the time between the vote and the effective date of the merger, each firm should operate normally, but neither should undertake any change in operations that would materially affect billings, collections, payment of expenses, lateral hires, or other operations without consulting with and getting approval from the other. Conflict checking is the exception, as this area needs to be handled with extreme care. Potential conflicts should be cross-checked against both firms' systems, straight through the merger vote and effective date.

Building the New Culture

Development of a common culture begins during negotiations and evolves over a course of several years. No matter how compatible the firms are, changes will take place. The only time one firm's culture survives is when it acquires a considerably smaller firm. Even then, some change will no doubt occur.

Partners must be committed to making the merger work and be willing to accept the fact that the new firm will develop a new culture. They must make a conscious effort not to push their original firm's culture on the new firm. Others in the firm take their cues from partners; if partners are careful to avoid an "us versus them" attitude, others will follow. One of the biggest contributions partners can make to the integration process is to involve partners and associates from the other firm in their practices.

When two firms of similar size merge, there may be no prevailing culture, and it is human nature for the partners in each firm to try to perpetuate their own firm's culture because they are more comfortable with it. The management group will have to spend considerable time dealing with partners who develop this attitude. Unless one culture can be developed soon after the deal is consummated, the entire integration process will take longer.

When two firms in different cities merge, the integration problems are exacerbated by logistics. Even if a large firm has merged with a smaller firm in another city, multiple locations make everything harder. It takes longer for people to get to know one another. It takes longer for partners to feel comfortable delegating work to partners and associates in the other office. It is more difficult to integrate office systems and procedures. In addition, transferring people from one office to another, either to help the integration process or to satisfy practice needs, may be an added difficulty.

When the merged firm retains different locations in a common city, the firm experiences many of the same problems as when the firm is in different cities. In some ways, the situation may be more difficult when there are multiple offices in one city, as there may be a heightened expectation for immediate integration.

Plan for Integration

In addition to forging one culture, the integration plan must provide for a business environment that will produce better business development opportunities. The business integration plan should address not only how the firm will run itself, but also the marketing of the merged practice.

The integration process is considerably more time-consuming than the evaluation and negotiation processes. Even if done efficiently, accomplishing it takes between one and two years. Because of the time, energy, and commitment involved, some firms lose steam and never complete integration. As a result, they never achieve the synergy they expected. Those who remain committed to the process, however, are rewarded by meeting, and even exceeding, the goals for the merger.

A well-thought-out plan for business integration, with timetables and assigned responsibilities, makes a significant difference in how long integration takes and how effective the integration is. The integration plan should cover both short-term and long-term goals.

The short-term plan should project the first six to twelve months. The immediate goal must be to continue service to clients without interruption. In developing a short-term plan, the management group must ask a variety of questions:

- What must the firm do now to provide uninterrupted service to clients? How must resources be allocated to ensure that necessary support is being given to service existing clients? Is it necessary to transfer people from one location to another or from one department or practice group to another?
- Are there any additional decisions the firm must make to implement the management structure agreed on during the merger discussions? Specifically, should the firm transfer lawyers among offices to help integration?
- Which decisions were made by the merger committee, and which must be made now?
- What are the management priorities?
- What are the practice management priorities?
- What must be done to put a practice management structure in place?
- Have all decisions concerning compensation for partners, associates, and staff been handled for the first year of operation?
- What must be done to draft and execute new firm agreements? Must any additional decisions be made about withdrawal issues (death, disability, retirement, voluntary withdrawal, and expulsion)?
- What committees should be appointed to help in the integration process?
- What business development efforts should be undertaken immediately? What action plans are necessary to achieve obvious business opportunities?

The merged firm's long-term strategic plan ultimately determines whether the combined firm gets the synergy expected from the merger. The strategic plan sets the direction for the firm's future practice. Any pre-merger strategic plan of either firm is no longer pertinent, although a pre-merger plan may help in the planning process. It may, however, be unrealistic to expect the firm to do extensive long-term planning at the outset. Most of the first year must be spent integrating the firm and the practice. Client integration must be supported by specific marketing strategies. While the firm may not have a formal long-range plan in place as it begins its integration process, it should have specific goals for integration. As the lawyers in the practice groups work together to integrate the practices and the clients, they discuss future goals and objectives that can form the basis for a strategic plan for the new firm.

Leadership and Management

Much has been written about the difference between leadership and management, and although it is not this book's purpose to debate that particular issue, the two roles should be differentiated. Leaders anticipate change and provide vision, influence, and guidance. They have gained the respect of their peers, who value their judgment and wisdom. Managers, in contrast, have responsibility for conducting the affairs of a business along a prescribed course. In some firms the leaders and managers are the same people; in other firms the leaders leave management to others. Partners who were leaders in the former firms must provide leadership in the new firm. They can, and should, set an example of effective communication and team play, even if they are not involved in day-to-day management.

Strong leadership is the key ingredient needed to turn two firms into one, even if the two firms passed every test of compatibility. Some differences in the two cultures always exist. It is critical, therefore, that leadership know how to manage those differences. Communication, consensus building, tolerance, opportunities for input about the new structure, and "management by walking the halls" are all essential.

Internal Communication

Communication must be a priority for the management group. This challenge is a formidable one in mergers of all sizes. The level of communication needed to make partners, associates, and staff comfortable in their new firm and with their new colleagues takes enormous time and energy.

A good rule during the transition period is to give people more information, rather than less. If management is open with information, people will feel more secure. In addition, management should actively seek ideas and provide an easy way for people to express their concerns. Creating the opportunity for people to build personal relationships through working together will increase their comfort level.

If practice group leaders visit each partner individually (and they should), the leader will have the opportunity to make the partner more comfortable about his or her role in the combined firm. It will also give the leader clues about what most concerns that particular partner, whether it is a personal concern or one that involves practice management or marketing. Not only does such a meeting enhance communication, but the practice group leader gets to know the partners in the group and solicit ideas for planning and marketing strategies for the group.

Partners from each firm should plan visits to major clients immediately after the merger. This is a priority. Clients must be assured that service will not be interrupted and that the firm is now in a better position to be more responsive than ever. These visits will not be a surprise to clients, since the client managers will have discussed the potential merger with them during the merger evaluation process.

Associates, paralegals, and staff will require attention. Meetings and social functions help integration, as does soliciting input from staff on administrative changes. Management should inform everyone about new policies regarding hours, compensation, benefits, and other factors in the workplace. These people may have worked under different values and expectations and may need time to understand and accept a new system.

Practice Management

Effective practice management may contribute more to integration, profitability, and synergy than any other single factor. If the lawyers in the new firm have confidence in the ability of their new partners and associates and are willing to work together and draw on each other's talents, the chances of success are enhanced greatly.

Leadership plays an important role in practice integration. Sharing clients and work is a primary reason for merger. Still, it is natural for the lawyers to hesitate to share clients and work with people they've never worked with before. The reluctance to hand over work to others may be eased somewhat as a result of having practice meetings between the groups before the lawyers actually move in together. Unfortunately, in some mergers the two firms continue to practice as they always have, and the practices are never really integrated. This result defeats the reason for the merger in the first place.

Most communication must come at the practice level. In big firms, this means departments and practice groups; in smaller firms, it means lawyers who practice in the same areas. What will determine the success of the new firm is not the terms of the merger but the ability of the partners to practice law together *by integrating practices, sharing clients, and developing new business through joint efforts.* The practice level also is where planning for practice development must begin, determining what the practice strengths and weaknesses of each practice area are, where the potential synergy is, how to develop more business from existing clients, and how to attract new business.

Although the merger agreement may include an overall concept for practice management, the actual departmental or other practice management structure will probably not be refined until after the merger and will continue to be refined during integration. If the practice managers and structure have not been designated in the merger agreement, the management team must appoint department heads, practice group leaders, or both to take responsibility for integrating the practices. In some instances, particularly when there are strong departments in each firm, two people may have responsibility for integrating the two former groups. A departmental structure serves as a vehicle for merging the practices. The merging process begins with an assessment of several important topics.

Lawyer Expertise

Although each firm will have a good idea of the overall expertise of its individual practitioners, that information is not enough to merge the practices properly. Department heads need to know not only the expertise of the lawyers, but also the amount of experience they have and examples of the actual cases, transactions, or projects each has handled. Once department heads have this information, they ensure that other lawyers in the firm know what others can do.

An important aspect of integration is educating partners about the expertise of the other lawyers in the firm. Success stories (summaries of cases and matters the firm has handled that show how the firm's expertise has helped a particular client) can be particularly useful. Meetings, however, are probably the best vehicle for teaching partners about the skills, expertise, and knowledge of others. Practice groups should meet weekly to discuss current work being done, the way that work got into the firm, any special needs dictated by that work, and the additional opportunities that might result. In addition, for the first year, various partners should be called on to discuss cases or matters they handled previously that will help educate others about what they can do.

As the partners get to know each other, they should become more comfortable involving each other in their work. The practice group leaders must play a major role here in encouraging such involvement, making specific suggestions on how to involve others.

Lawyer Workload

Making staffing changes and reallocating workloads is a sensitive issue, to clients as well as to lawyers. To the extent necessary, the lawyers, and in some instances the clients, should be part of the decision-making process. It is not a good idea to make any changes unless they are absolutely necessary. Usually, a merged firm begins to shift work around slowly because continuity with the client is critical.

If one firm is overloaded, then reshuffling work may be fairly painless. To be effective with clients, however, the firm may have to bear the expense of making new lawyers knowledgeable about particular clients. Most often, partners in the merged firm begin to share work with one another as new work comes in. The client manager should discuss with the client the added expertise and resources that will be available to the client through the merger. In this situation as well, the firm may have to bear the expense of educating lawyers about the client's business.

Relocation of lawyers can be a key to effective integration. It is best if the lawyer(s) relocating are key lawyers in the firm. Relocation can help with the day-to-day integration but should also be based on client or practice needs. In some cases, relocated lawyers can serve as the starting point for future practice growth.

An alternative to relocation is to have a designated lawyer with the needed expertise spend some time in an office. This arrangement may broaden the field of lawyers available. Lawyers in that office can "sell" services on the basis of that lawyer's expertise and the fact that he or she spends considerable time in the office and can charge expenses such as travel out of the office with which the client normally deals.

Departmental Structure

In large firms one trend is toward relatively large departments with small practice groups within each department. For example, the firm might have a litigation department, with practice groups in general business litigation, antitrust, product liability, intellectual property, and so forth. A business department might have practice groups in real estate, tax, estate planning, general corporate, franchising, and so forth. With this type of structure, management is divided into more manageable units. A department head operates as a managing partner of that department, and practice group leaders report to the department heads. Communication and marketing are usually improved because smaller groups of people can meet more informally and know more about each other's workloads, expertise, and clients. In some instances, a practice group may be designated for a particular industry or client group. For example, a practice team that crosses several practice disciplines may be designated for a health care client.

Smaller firms still tend to be structured along broad practice lines such as litigation, real estate, business, tax, and the like.

There may be only one level of management. In very small firms the managing partner, a practice coordinator, or a designated member of the management committee usually supervises the practices.

The point is to have a structure that supports what the firm is trying to accomplish, makes client service better, ensures quality services, and makes cross-selling and marketing easier.

Meetings and Operations

Frequent practice group meetings during the first few months are critical, even if such meetings require travel and additional time commitments. In small firms the lawyers will meet more informally; it is not as critical to have formal meetings. When the firm is in more than one location, visits are extremely important.

Risk Management

Intake, conflict management, and quality control are a critical function in any firm and are particularly important after a merger. This function includes:

- ◆ *Work intake controls.* What remains to be done after the merger is to implement procedures, educate lawyers about those procedures, and give practice leaders a system for enforcing the policies.
- ◆ *Conflict procedures.* Once the merger has taken place, the firm needs a system for checking incoming matters for possible conflicts.
- ◆ *Opinion and audit letters.* Written procedures for both opinions and audits are important.

Associate Management

Communication

Regardless of how many associates are involved in the merger, they will be uneasy about it. Although they were aware of the merger negotiations and may have attended social functions, they will need a good deal of attention and information. By communicating to the associates how the firm intends to handle associate integration, the firm can ease their concerns and gain their support in the integration process. Discussions with associates should include compensation, partnership track, and opportunities for work.

Work Assignment

Work assignment to associates may change after the merger; the extent of change usually depends on the practices being merged. For example, if the merger is an acquisition of an environmental group, the associates in that group will no doubt continue to work with the same partners they were working with before the merger. If the merger brings in a group of lawyers who did not have enough work to do in their former firm, it is necessary to find work for them immediately.

In setting up the firm's practice management structure, the practice group leaders should develop guidelines for work assignment. The goal is to get work allocated in such a way that client needs are served (those come first), that partners get the associate support they need, and that associate workloads are as equalized as possible under the circumstances. At the same time, if partners perceive they have lost control of their own practices, those partners' fear and resentment may increase.

In most firms, partners assign work directly to associates without approval from a practice group leader, although there may be limits on which associates are free to take work assignments from which lawyers or groups of lawyers. If both firms operated this way in the past, the partners will be inclined to continue to assign work as they always have. In most situations, the practice group leaders will have to encourage partners to assign work to associates in the other firm. It is easier to accomplish this goal in a practice management structure that divides the practice into small practice groups within each department rather than have dozens of lawyers in one department. Even small firms can designate practice groups or teams of specified partners and associates.

Recruiting

Recruiting in small firms is not a major undertaking, and in a merger of small firms, recruiting efforts might not change significantly. In large firms, however, recruiting is a major endeavor. Most large firms employ full-time recruiting coordinators. It is increasingly common for large firms to have recruiting committees, with associates heavily involved, which handle all aspects of recruiting from initial contacts to hiring prospective associates. The integration of recruiting efforts is one area that can produce significant cost savings.

The management group or appropriate committee should review the standards for hiring new or lateral associates. Some firms maintain lists of approved schools or hire associates who graduated at a minimum rank level within their class—say, within the top 25 percent. Although these standards may have been reviewed and agreed on before the merger, it is more likely that this issue would be addressed after the merger. Agreeing on recruiting standards will help avoid future issues that could delay or halt recruiting efforts midseason.

Each firm should provide immediate notification of the merger to any students who have already been offered positions for the upcoming year. In some cases, a merger can significantly affect a firm's work atmosphere and thereby change the commitments made by students before the merger. Firms that maintain frequent communications with students who have accepted offers tend to have fewer problems in maintaining those individuals and integrating them into the newly created firm.

Training

Training tends to be one of the easiest areas to integrate in any merger. Surveys of partners and associates show that lawyer training is an area that almost always needs improvement. As a result, most existing training programs (if any) are generally welcomed into the newly merged firm. Once the programs are consolidated, each associate's training history must be documented to ensure that each associate goes through the entire training program.

Many firms use mentor programs, in which they assign a partner or senior associate to every new associate to provide better integration into the firm, improve training, and enhance professional development. If one of the firms has such a program in place, the program can be broadened to include associates from the other firm.

One aspect of training that is frequently overlooked is the transition for associates coming from a smaller firm into a larger firm. Associates in smaller firms frequently enjoy easy access to partners or more senior associates. Smaller firms also tend to have less-formal, more-personalized forms of training that can quickly disappear in the course of a merger. In addition, when merged into a larger firm, small-firm associates frequently become lost in the maze of departments and more formal assignments of lawyers. To ensure that this transition goes smoothly and that associates know where to turn for help, the firm should designate several partners to help in that transition.

Evaluation

A formal evaluation system for assessing associate performance must be developed. If one of the firms has an effective evaluation process, that process can be implemented for the merged firm. Associates need to know what is expected of them, what will be the basis on which they will be evaluated, and where they stand on the partnership track. For the first evaluation conducted after the merger, it may be necessary for partners to evaluate the associates from their original firm. This would be the case if there is little time between the merger and the evaluation. This approach should be used for one year only.

Partnership

In most mergers, admission to partnership is discussed during the negotiation process. This is especially true if one firm has a two-tier structure and the other does not. (See Chapter 4.) In a small merger, it is relatively easy for all partners to have the opportunity to work with the few associates who might be considered for promotion shortly after the merger date. In large mergers, the practice group leaders should see to it that senior associates are given the opportunity to work with partners from the other firm. In the final analysis, however, it may be necessary to rely on the recommendation of the partners from the associate's firm as to when that associate is ready for partnership.

Compensation

Aligning associate compensation systems is usually addressed during the merger discussions. The key is to understand what the firm wants to accomplish through compensation, and then to develop a system around those goals. Some firms use merger as an opportunity to revamp their entire compensation process. It is important to recognize the need to align approaches early, as associates who believe they aren't being treated equitably will quickly become disgruntled.

Capital Structure

Future financial planning involves the issues of capitalization and debt. As part of the firm's strategic planning process, the firm must assess the proper mix and levels of debt and capital that will be needed to implement its plan. Factors influencing this decision include current debt levels and the availability of additional external financing. The decision whether to borrow or to require additional funds to be paid in by partners will be based on the firm's current financial position and its long-term strategy.

Many well-managed firms prepare formal capital plans that project capital requirements, including significant asset additions, over a three- to five-year period. Once the firm knows its total capital requirements, it can plan for increased partner capital requirements or increased debt.

Partner Compensation

In some mergers of large firms, each prior firm sets partner compensation for partners of that firm for the first year of the merger. It is preferable not to extend this practice beyond the first year. The rationale for this approach is that it is impossible for the partners in one group to understand completely the contributions of the partners in the other firm. To speed up the education process, it may be desirable to have representatives from each group observe the compensation process of the other group. Once the partners begin to practice together and there is both a management structure and a practice management structure in place to help evaluate contributions, the need for setting compensation in two groups should dissipate. In smaller firms, it may not be necessary to employ an interim step. Rather, the two leadership groups work together to arrive at appropriate compensation levels for the partners.

If the compensation system does not include a bonus pool of some type, a bonus pool may be desirable for the transition process. This approach will allow the firm to make adjustments when a partner's performance significantly exceeds expectations.

Physical Integration

If the merger is between firms in the same city, or with offices in the same city, the goal should be for the new firm to consolidate into one location as soon as possible. If that is impossible, then people should be moved around so that there are a substantial number of people from each firm in each location. This can be accomplished by assigning all people in one department or practice group to the same location. It is important to have a target date for physical consolidation.

Publicizing and Marketing the Merger

In making its decision to seek the merger, each firm should have spent substantial time analyzing its client base and clients' industries for increased marketing opportunities. For the combined firm to reach its potential, the majority of partners must spend significant time exploring opportunities created by the combination. This time must be added to the time that has already been spent negotiating the merger. There is no way to estimate how much time these activities will take. It is safe to say, however, that time spent in marketing activities (and firm integration) must be *in addition* to the time partners have spent working with clients. (The possible exceptions are for partners in major management positions.) Marketing the merged firm can be divided into two major categories:

1. Public relations efforts that must be handled immediately.
2. Marketing that will begin immediately but will continue beyond the integration of the two firms.

Public Relations

Both firms will probably have dealt with the news media by the time the merger is finalized and should have agreed that there will be a small number of representatives speaking to the media regarding the merger. Once the merger decision is made, however, it is essential to have a well-thought-out public relations approach. Exhibit 22 on pages 168–170 is a public relations checklist.

Designated Spokesperson

One of the first decisions that must be made after the merger is whether the same person from each firm will continue to be the designated spokesperson. If the firm has more than one office, there should be a designated spokesperson from each office to address local inquiries. The spokespersons must agree on the specific points that should be made in publicity and marketing efforts. Partners with a national, regional, or state presence or widespread name recognition serve well in this role.

Each spokesperson should have the same specific information about both of the prior firms and the new firm. This can be done through the preparation of a fact sheet giving general information that the news media will ask about each firm as well as about the combined firm. (See Exhibit 23 on pages 171–172 for a sample.) The fact sheets should contain information that can be distributed universally.

People in the firm should be advised, either by memo or through meetings, who the official spokespersons are and what official information can be divulged when they are asked about the merger. Any questions regarding information not in the memo should be referred to official spokespersons. If there is to be a press conference to announce the merger, everyone in the firm should be told before the press conference.

Information Package

It is helpful to prepare an information package containing the fact sheets previously described, copies of press releases about the merger, published articles about the firms, firm brochures, and other promotional materials. These packages can be used for overall public relations efforts and also for visits to clients and prospective clients.

Communication with Clients

Someone must be responsible for determining which clients require personal visits and scheduling meetings with those clients. Implementation of visits, telephone calls, or mailings is usually delegated to various partners. In large firms, the marketing department coordinates all marketing activities. Once the firms decide to merge, they should agree on the date to notify key clients, the date to notify all clients, and the date to notify the press. Personal visits are the best way to inform key clients. Visits to key clients may have been made before the merger is announced; in that event, clients must be asked to keep the merger announcement confidential. Second visits to some key clients may be appropriate after the merger is announced.

For visits to clients, preparation is a key. Partners who make the visits should be prepared to discuss the benefits that the client will receive from the merger. They should also anticipate client concerns and questions and be prepared to answer them. In large firms marketing staff are heavily involved in such preparation.

Other clients may be informed by telephone, and some in writing. For clients who will be informed by telephone, someone must be given the specific responsibility for notifying a definitive list of clients, along with some guidance about what information to give. The individual lawyers given the responsibility may follow up in writing.

For clients who will be informed by letter, it is necessary to take several steps:

♦ Approve the text of the letter.
♦ Prepare the mailing lists.
♦ Decide who (the managing partner, responsible partners, etc.) will sign the letters.
♦ Decide what additional information about the firm will be sent with the letter.
♦ Determine the earliest date clients should receive the letters (vis-à-vis press publicity).

The letter should describe the benefits that clients will receive from the merger and should anticipate and allay client concerns about the merger. It may be necessary to have multiple versions of the letter for each firm, for different offices, and for different types of clients. To the extent possible, the letter should fit the circumstance.

Media Coverage

The merger committee, and the consultant if one is involved, should have a plan that includes simultaneous release to the press that will be notified. The press release should be ready when the merger decision is made. The press that will be contacted depends on the size of the merger, but the plan for press releases must include both the media that will be contacted personally and those that will simply be sent press releases. The spokesperson should categorize the press by national general press, national business press, national legal press, local general press, local business press, and relevant trade publications (vis-à-vis practice specialties).

Providing the press with information and answering questions will produce much more positive stories than will a secretive approach. Remember that the merger will be old news quickly. Capitalize on what makes the merger newsworthy. Has either firm been involved in a high-profile case recently? What does the combined firm hope to accomplish from the merger?

If the merger is important enough for a press conference, lawyers need to be prepared for the conference. Exhibit 24 on page

173 shows a checklist of typical questions that can be used to help prepare for a press conference.

Other Forms of Announcement

Public relations efforts also typically include a formal announcement to clients, business acquaintances, and referral sources. Most firms plan social events, such as open houses, to help introduce the new firm to clients, referral sources, and the business community.

Marketing the Practice

Marketing efforts should include firmwide efforts (brochures, announcements, open houses, visibility in the community, etc.), but the most effective marketing will be that done at the practice level by the individual lawyers. This is why a good practice management structure with strong leadership is so important. Although the firm may appoint a business development and marketing committee to help launch a marketing program with the support of the marketing committee, the department heads should play a primary role in marketing.

A major goal is to educate clients about the added depth and expertise provided by the merger. The firm will achieve its goal more readily if it uses an organized approach to marketing the expanded services the firm can provide. Although marketing principles are the same in many businesses, in a merged firm it makes sense to focus on marketing strategies that will educate the lawyers, clients, and prospective clients about what the combined firm has to offer.

Communication with clients from the first day that the combined firm begins work is critical. Each partner should develop a list of contacts that he or she intends to make to clients. Firm members should also talk to clients about their needs and how the firm can enhance its service and responsiveness.

The marketing committee, with support from the marketing department, should analyze the type of work each firm has been doing, categorized by practice area, for its clients. (Begin with the biggest revenue producers and work down.) The committee should also identify by practice area the types of work either firm has done for the client. This gives the firm a picture of the types of work that can now be marketed to the client.

The new firm should identify client industries in which either firm has been doing significant work so that it can take advantage of targeting specific industries. One partner might be charged with the responsibility for showcasing expertise in a specific industry.

Department heads should work together and with the marketing committee and marketing department to discuss how the departments can cross-sell each other (and other office locations, if there are any). An effective approach is to designate client or industry teams of lawyers from various practice disciplines. These types of interdisciplinary teams should be discussed in marketing meetings so that all lawyers become educated about the approach.

If the firm has merged to achieve regional expansion, the firm should identify the opportunities available from the merger. A marketing plan should be developed for each office.

Some of the firm's lawyers may need marketing training, in which case the firm should provide that training, either with other lawyers in the firm or by retaining outside help. Marketing is not a one-time project. It is an ongoing process that requires knowledge and information about clients and their industries. The firm must be able to anticipate clients' needs. Clients expect it.

The firm should have a written marketing plan with a list of marketing goals that the firm expects to achieve for the coming year. Each department and practice group should have written marketing goals. Most importantly, each year all partners and associates should develop, with the assistance of their department head or practice group leader (or managing partner if the firm is small), specific marketing goals as part of their individual planning process. The firm's marketing department should initiate and coordinate all marketing activities.

Integrating Administration and Technology

10

Introduction

Communication is key in the integration of support services. Staff are understandably anxious about the merger. They need communication early and often. Although the administrative and technological issues are not typically deal breakers in merger discussions, a merged firm that does not plan adequately for integration in these areas is asking for trouble. Most firms are careful to have a plan for integrating the partners and associates, but they put off the support systems and staff until after the merger. They avoid the tough decisions that must be made in both administrative and technological matters, which leads to poor staff morale, high turnover, and general confusion and misinformation among the administrative staff. This, in turn, can lead to poor support services and ultimately poor service to the firm's clients.

The plan for the integration should be in place at the time the firms vote to become one firm.

Administrative Management Structure

The firm's administrative structure must flow from its management structure. The purpose of the administrative structure is to complement firm management and to provide lawyers with the administrative and technological support they need to do client work. Even if one or both of the administrative structures were effective for the prior firms before merger, they may not be appropriate for the new firm. In many cases, a totally new administrative structure must be developed to accommodate the new firm size and structure.

Once a structure has been designed for the new firm, management must determine if any of the old positions from the two firms can be incorporated into the new structure.

A more difficult issue is whether the individuals filling the current administrative positions and the administrators themselves can fit into the new firm. Whether the combined firm will need both administrators beyond the integration stage depends on the size of the combined firm, the administrative structure agreed on, and the qualifications of the administrators themselves. The firms must also deal with other duplications in administrative supervisory staff and support staff. These staff issues are the most difficult for firm management to address. However, if these personnel issues are not dealt with early, they will be more difficult to deal with later, after major problems, bad feelings, and poor morale develop.

To begin the process of evaluating which personnel might fit into which slot, each firm should prepare an organizational chart identifying each administrative function, supervisory and staff positions related to each function, and reporting lines. Every position should be listed with a written description of all tasks and responsibilities, as well as job authority. The salary and benefits package for each position also must be listed. (This information will be used for the pro forma budget as well.) Key staff members often agree to stay through the merger integration, even if their positions may be eliminated.

It is not unusual for the new firm to have higher administrative support ratios than the ratios of the two individual firms before the merger. This is particularly true in office services (mail, messenger, housekeeping, photocopying), information services and systems, records, and library services. Because each firm often brings its own administrative and office services staff, there will be duplication for a while. The duplication can be helpful during the transition into one firm. At some point, the ratios stabilize either through attrition or because the firm increases in size without adding administrative staff. If the ratios do not stabilize within a reasonable time, it may be necessary to cut some staff positions.

A merger can also be an opportunity for both firms to maximize the efficiency of the support services. Some firms are starting to centralize support services, increasingly in off-site locations. This has particular appeal as part of a merger because it can eliminate the "home office" concept that is fast fading in large multioffice firms.

Administrative Policies and Procedures

Dealing with firm policies and operating procedures is just as difficult and emotional an issue as dealing with personnel decisions. Each firm's policies and procedures must be reviewed to determine which, if any, will be appropriate for the new firm. The administrators (or designated members of the administrative staff) of the two firms can work together to develop a proposal for management. Both lawyers and staff should be given the opportunity to make suggestions at some point in the process. Exhibit 25 on pages 174–176 provides a discussion agenda.

Because the merged firm is a combination of two different firms, it is vital that it provide written and consistently enforced policies and procedures. Support staff will be apprehensive about the changes they expect from the merger, and written guidelines will go a long way toward reassuring them, particularly if they are given the opportunity to provide suggestions and ask questions about the policies and procedures.

In addition, the larger the firm, the more important it is to establish written, formal guidelines on how the firm will operate and how personnel-related issues will be handled. These include firmwide policies about issues such as benefits, vacation and holidays, sick time, and performance reviews, as well as descriptions of various administrative support services and such procedures as office services, accounting, and the like. In addition, most insurance carriers require that firms have formal, written procedures for protecting against potential conflicts of interest, for managing cases, and for tracking files. Combining two firms dramatically increases the need for attention to these matters.

Administrative Staffing

Another policy issue that must be addressed includes who will supervise, hire, fire, train, and evaluate the support staff. Compensation and benefits plans must be developed, and someone has to administer them. The two firms may have handled these issues differently, and management must provide a consistent plan for the new firm. In a smaller firm an office manager may have these responsibilities. In larger firms these duties may be divided among several positions. A general administrator may have overall responsibility for all firm administrative matters, but the daily tasks and duties associated with some of these matters may be handled by one or more specialists. For example, a personnel manager may be responsible for all human resources hiring, firing, and performance evaluation. A benefits specialist may be responsible for administering the firm's benefits programs.

Administrative Services

The new firm is often much larger, but firm management may not recognize that some of the support functions must be expanded to meet the increased demands. This is particularly true in the office services areas, such as mail and messenger, photocopying, facilities management and office maintenance, and files and records management. It also pertains to billing and accounting, collections, and library services.

Some of these areas may be expanded into separate operational departments. This is especially true of facilities management and records management. Maintaining the firm's physical plant (office maintenance, furniture/fixed assets, office renovations, and moves) is an important and time-consuming function that must be handled by trained people.

Records management—which includes maintenance of all firm files; management of file staff; oversight of file opening, closing, and retention procedures; and oversight of the firmwide conflict of interest system—is a specialized and important function in firms of all sizes. Merged firms in particular must integrate their file systems into one that will work for the new firm. This integration includes a consistent system for file naming and numbering, a firmwide conflict of interest system, and firmwide file-tracking procedures.

Smaller firms may not have individual people responsible for these functions. These functions are critical, however, and someone must be responsible and accountable for them. In smaller firms, the administrator or office services supervisor may handle all of these functions. In larger firms, more specially trained people will be necessary to oversee these functions, particularly in the short term.

Information Technology

The integration of technology is often one of the more significant expenses associated with a merger. This includes upgrades of one firm's technology platform to make it compatible; conversion of financial systems, document management, and key practice and support systems; and training in new systems. A merger is also an opportunity for both firms to evaluate their strategic technology plans and determine if the needs of the combined firm will require investment in technical tools that neither firm currently has.

First, each firm involved in the merger must inventory all its information technology (IT) resources, from the IT organization itself to its reference materials, equipment, vendor contracts, and projects in process. Firm management must determine the following:

◆ Are there "holes" in the systems portfolio of either firm that will need to be filled for the new firm? Sometimes, the whole is greater than the sum of the parts. In other words, either firm on its own may not have been able to justify expensive practice-specific or systems management software. If the new firm is planning to promote and develop a specific practice to leverage the newly joined resources or if the new firm's IT infrastructure becomes geometrically more complex, new systems may be required. These new systems require planning, acquisition, design, training, and implementation time and expense. These may significantly affect the new firm's ability to consolidate technical as well as functional resources.

◆ Are the core systems in each firm's systems portfolio compatible? Can front- and back-office information (documents, document management data, financial management data, calendars, e-mail, and address books) be transferred easily between the systems? What are the costs associated with staffing and setting up temporary OCR scanning equipment and developing or acquiring special conversion programs for word processing, document management, e-mail, and financial management systems? These items must be considered in the pro forma budget. Of particular concern is the conversion of records from the legacy firms' time and billing/financial management systems into the new firm's system. The cost of data conversion and personnel training can be considerable.

◆ Are there other mismatches in the systems portfolios of the two firms? How will they be reconciled to achieve a single, integrated systems architecture for the new firm? Besides a firm's core systems, there are system and network utility software packages that are designed to keep the firm's computers free of viruses, back up critical data, and facilitate PC desktop configuration, among others. It is inefficient and expensive to maintain two different sets of software to perform the same function. While there may not be an immediate requirement to consolidate to a single standard software package, plans and budgets should be developed to address any such redundancy.

◆ Can any of the existing systems be expanded or upgraded to handle the increased volumes of the new firm? For example, one firm may have a superior intellectual property management system that runs well in a local office, but the new firm may need to have that system networked to handle twice the number of records and users in multiple locations. This may require significant upgrade costs for the software itself as well as for network infrastructure. Time also is a significant element in this planning exercise. The upgrade may take months, and interim contingency plans will need to be developed.

If neither of the existing systems can be expanded or upgraded, a third system must be selected and prepared for installation and conversion. This will be a major undertaking in terms of conversion, training, and deployment. These types of projects should have ample funds budgeted for outsourced integration and implementation services, not only on the technical side but also on the functional side (administration). The firm's staff may be too busy managing the daily operational aspects of the merger to undertake a project of this magnitude that will, undoubtedly, have a fixed or tight deadline for completion.

◆ When must each of the two firms' systems be merged? How soon must the new firm use one billing and one conflict-checking system? The answer typically is "as soon as possible," but it may not be practical for any number of reasons. Causes of a delay include the time to effect a conversion from one system to the other (if there are different systems), the time to effect an upgrade of the preferred system to accommodate the new volumes, the time to work out a standard set of operating procedures for the new firm, and simply enough, the time to wait until a new fiscal year begins.

- ◆ How are both firms using, managing, and supporting their information technology? If one firm is a leading-edge user of technology, it will have a high ratio of IT support staff and IT-related expense to users (and, it is hoped, be receiving appropriate value from them). If the other firm is a trailing-edge or middle-of-the-road user, it may balk at these high support and development costs. In today's technological world, these costs can be significant—up to 5 or 6 percent of a firm's annual revenue.

In addition to the specific hardware and software, management must review basic front- and back-office work flow processes. For example, will the new firm have a centralized billing function, or will some bill-processing capabilities be distributed to secretaries and other staff members in each office location? Management must also determine what other practice support or management functions must be adjusted or expanded to meet the needs of the new firm. The best way to address these issues is to step through the complete life cycle of a typical matter from file opening (including docketing, conflict checking, and records management) to file closing and determine what systems, support staff, and network links will be required to process these everyday transactions for the new firm in a timely and efficient manner.

Decisions involving administration and technology can be very difficult, especially when positions may be eliminated or changed, or computer systems and long-standing procedures may be scrapped. If one system must be chosen over another, the new firm must try to avoid rivalry between systems personnel. One way to accomplish this is through an independent third party who can help the new firm make an objective decision. It is important that the administrative staff and the technology systems be integrated as soon as possible to promote the "one firm" atmosphere, cut costs, and ensure that staff and technology are utilized effectively to meet clients' needs.

Exhibit 1
PRACTICE DEVELOPMENT QUESTIONNAIRE

1. What are the strengths in your practice area?
2. What are you doing to capitalize on these strengths?
3. What are the weaknesses in your practice area?
4. What are you doing to address these weaknesses?
5. What is your present client base (identify key clients) and its source? This includes the services you are currently providing key clients, the nature of the workload, and the long-term projection for this type of work.
6. What areas of practice do or could complement your practice area? What areas complement your clients?
7. What would be a complementary base? What type of client matters would you like to see the firm practice?
8. Describe current cross-selling in your firm. What could be done to improve cross-selling in your firm?
9. What do you do to market your personal practice? To market your practice group? To market the firm generally?
10. What are your practice group's marketing or business development priorities?
11. What are the practice area's staffing needs to meet present and projected workload? What needs do your clients have that you are not able to service? How best can your practice staff be complemented?
12. How can the profitability of your practice area be enhanced?
13. What are the firm's plans for expanding the practice area?
14. What are the long-term prospects for your practice area? How does this coincide with your long-term vision of the firm?
15. What other growth areas of the firm should be expanded?
16. What areas are not profitable or should be reduced or culled?
17. In a firm merger, what are or would be the concerns of the lawyers within your practice area?

Exhibit 2
FIRST MEETING AGENDA

Note: See calendar of events (Exhibit 4).

I. Initial discussion
   A. Firm history
   B. Practice areas and client representation
      1. Brief profile of practice
      2. Brief profile of key clients
      3. Discussion of potential conflicts
   C. Reasons why each firm is considering merger
      1. Firm's strengths and weaknesses
      2. What the firm brings to the table
      3. Cross-selling opportunities with existing clients
      4. Opportunities to develop new clients
      5. Goals and direction for the future
      6. Combined firm's position in the marketplace
   D. Each firm's approach to key issues
      1. Partnership structure
      2. Management
      3. Partner compensation system
      4. Practice management/departmentalization
      5. Business development and marketing
   E. Reasons to continue discussions, or not
   F. Game plan for merger evaluation (See Exhibit 3)

Exhibit 3
STRATEGIC MERGER CHECKLIST

Note: See calendar of events (Exhibit 4).

I.   Initial discussion (See Exhibit 2 for first meeting agenda)
II. Development of game plan for merger evaluation
    A. Discuss and outline the evaluation process.
    B. Select a merger committee (3–5 participants) to represent each firm.
    C. Discuss role and utilization of outside help.
       1. Consultants
       2. Accounting firm
    D. Appoint subcommittees to assist with the process.
       1. Conflicts
       2. Finance
       3. Partner compensation
       4. Partner retirement, welfare, and benefits plans
       5. Practice group coordinators
       6. Associate management and recruiting
       7. Marketing and public relations
       8. Technology and systems integration
       9. Administration and integration
    E. Develop master calendar.
       1. Assignment of responsibilities
       2. Timetables for completion
       3. Schedule for additional meetings
    F. Exchange financial information.
       1. Information to be exchanged
       2. Who will be responsible for the analysis
    G. Exchange client lists for conflicts checks.
    H. Plan communication to partners and social gathering.
    I. Develop merger notebook.
III. Discussion of key issues
    A. Firm name
    B. Partnership structure
       1. Lawyer classifications and descriptions; leverage

2. Admission criteria
3. Track
4. Number of upcoming partner candidates
5. Outstanding commitments and special arrangements
6. Admission of lateral partners
7. Potential loss of partners
8. Partner age distribution

C. Firm governance
  1. Firm management
     a. Decisions reserved to the partners
     b. Voting requirements
  2. Firm chair/managing partner
     a. Method of selection
     b. Term of office
     c. Responsibilities and authority
     d. Client responsibilities
     e. Compensation arrangement
  3. Management/executive committee
     a. Method of selection
     b. Term of office
     c. Responsibilities and authority
     d. Time commitment
  4. Compensation committee
     a. Method of selection
     b. Term of office
     c. Responsibilities and authority
  5. Other standing committees
     a. Names and functions of committees
     b. Method of selection
     c. Responsibilities and authority
  6. Practice structure
     a. Departments
     b. Method of management
     c. Multioffice practice management
     d. Cross-departmental and industry groups
  7. Office management
     a. Office managing partner

      i. Method of selection

      ii. Responsibilities and authority

   b. Administration

      i. Firm administrative structure

         (a) Organization chart

         (b) Role of the executive director

      ii. Office administrative structure

8. Partner compensation, retirement, and benefits

   a. Compensation philosophy

      i. Criteria considered, relative importance of each

      ii. Open vs. closed results

   b. Compensation system

      i. System to be used in the combined firm

      ii. System for integration period

   c. Who sets compensation

      i. Decision makers

      ii. Involvement of partners

      iii. Voting/approval process, if any

   d. Method for setting compensation

      i. Timing—prospective or retrospective

      ii. Points, percentages, or other

      iii. Bonus pool

      iv. Draw policy

      v. Frequency of setting compensation

   e. Capital requirements

      i. Paid-in capital requirement

      ii. Method of payment

      iii. Payout terms

      iv. Integration of two approaches

9. Retirement policies

   a. Mandatory retirement age

   b. Early retirement option

   c. Phasedown option/requirement

   d. Funded/unfunded plan

10. Partner perquisites

   a. Business development and entertainment

   b. Dues and seminars

  c. Pension and welfare benefit plans

  d. Reimbursement policies

 11. Withdrawal policies

  a. Voluntary

  b. Involuntary

 12. Disability policies and benefits

  a. Short term

  b. Long term

  c. Insurance requirements

 13. Death benefits

  a. Key man insurance

  b. Special arrangements

IV. Financial analysis

 A. Comparable historical analysis

 B. Preparation of pro forma budgets and cash flow projections

  1. Projected merger costs and savings

  2. Benefit of potential synergies

 C. Capitalization and debt structure

 D. Off-balance-sheet items, including lease obligations and unfunded payments to former and retired partners

 E. Economic balance sheet

 F. Accounting year

 G. Tax issues

 H. Billing and collection policies

  1. Work-in-process valuation

  2. Accounts receivable valuation

 I. Method and timing of combination

 J. Borrowing philosophy

 K. Banking relationship

 L. Hourly billing rate comparison and assessment of realization

 M. Tax structure (PC, partnership/LLP)

V. Client conflicts

 A. Evaluation of direct conflicts

 B. Evaluation of indirect conflicts

 C. Examination of referral sources

 D. Conflicts checking system during merger discussions

VI. Professional liability insurance
- A. Insurance carrier
- B. Retention and limits
- C. Prior acts coverage
- D. History of claims
- E. Outstanding claims and potential exposure

VII. General firm policies
- A. Acceptance of cases
  1. Approval requirements
  2. Contingent matters
  3. Alternative pricing arrangements
  4. Pro bono matters
- B. Philosophy of work
  1. Billable hour requirements
  2. Approved nonbillable categories
- C. Bar association activities
  1. Commitment of time
  2. Reimbursement of costs
- D. Contributions
  1. Political
  2. Charitable
- E. Personnel policies
  1. Vacation
  2. Sabbatical program
  3. Maternity/paternity
  4. Part-time arrangements
  5. Nepotism
- F. Associate management
  1. Recruiting program
     a. Hiring from law schools
     b. Policy on lateral hiring
     c. Current offers outstanding
  2. Training program
     a. Department assignments
     b. Case assignment system
     c. Mentor program
  3. Evaluation process

      a. Methodology

      b. Frequency

      c. Timing of salary adjustments

   4. Compensation philosophy

      a. Salary

      b. Bonus system

      c. Branch office policies

G. Quality control

   1. Audit and opinion letters

   2. Acceptance of business

H. Administration and operations

   1. Personnel policies and benefits

      a. Health and benefits plans

      b. Employee vs. firm contribution

      c. Retirement benefits

      d. 401k

         i. Matching contributions

        ii. Investment options

   2. Accounting procedures and policies

   3. Facilities and equipment

   4. Office insurance coverage

I. Information systems integration

   1. Hardware/software used

   2. Desktop systems/laptop policy

      a. Accounting system

      b. Telephone/voice mail

   3. Long-term capital plan/lease vs. buy philosophy

   4. Integration issues

Exhibit 4
CALENDAR OF EVENTS

1. First meeting   Within 30 days of
                                    introduction
2. Financial evaluations   30–60 days
3. Meeting of merger committee,   45 days
   discussion of numbers and key
   issues
4. Social gathering of partners   60 days
5. Conflicts check   Initial: To be completed
                                    within 60 days. Also,
                                    continued checks on all
                                    new clients/matters during
                                    evaluation process.
6. Practice group meetings   45–90 days
7. Second meeting of merger   60–75 days
   committee, resolution of key
   issues
8. Preliminary reports of   105–120 days
   subcommittees
9. Third meeting of merger   120–135 days
   committee, continued
   resolution of key issues
10. Fourth meeting of merger   135–150 days
    committee, final report of
    committees, final resolution of
    all issues, discussion of
    presentation to partners
11. Final draft of merger notebook 165–180 days
12. Fifth meeting of merger   180 days
    committee, review of notebook
13. Notebook distribution and   195 days
    information meetings of the
    partners
14. Formal vote   210 days

Exhibit 5
MERGER COMMITTEE

I. General responsibilities
   A. Coordinate all merger activities, analyses, and negotiations, and propose final recommendations on terms of the merger before submission for partnership approval.

II. Specific responsibilities
   A. Propose firm name.
   B. Appoint subcommittees as needed to study discrete issues.
   C. Act on recommendations made by merger subcommittees.
   D. Determine level of financial information to be distributed to the partners.
   E. Establish the partners' compensation arrangements.
   F. Finalize method of merger.
      1. Method of combining assets
      2. Valuation of assets, including work in progress and accounts receivable
      3. Direction to each firm regarding billing and collections before merger
      4. Method of dissolving and/or combining partnership and professional corporation
   G. Choose members of executive committee.
   H. Appoint practice integration committee.
   I. Define responsibilities of other groups.
      1. Executive committee
      2. Department heads and practice group leaders
      3. Administrator
      4. Other committees
   J. Appoint post-merger committee, if different from merger committee.
   K. Develop procedures for press releases and communications with the news media, determine form of announcement, and designate spokespersons to coordinate all public relations functions. (Merger committee may delegate

development of procedures to spokespersons to coordinate public relations.)

L. Make decision concerning liabilities to former partners.

M. Prepare forecasts.

Exhibit 6
MERGER FINANCE SUBCOMMITTEE

I. Financial analysis (income statement, balance sheet, cash flows, capital budgets)
    A. Compare economic results.
    B. Prepare summary on comparable basis.
    C. Compare partner compensation.
II. Pro forma projections for first year
    A. Prepare budget for coming year as starting point.
    B. Make adjustments to combined budget.
    C. Develop multiyear projection.
III. Resolution of key issues
    A. Determine method of combination, considering legal and tax aspects.
       1. Pooling of interests
       2. Purchase
       3. Starting a new firm
       4. Other
    B. Determine liabilities and debt.
       1. Identify liabilities, including off-balance-sheet items such as operating leases and unfunded retirement obligations.
       2. Determine responsibility for payment.
       3. Handle liabilities to former partners.
    C. Propose capitalization.
       1. Credit of partners' capital accounts at date of merger
       2. Future capital expenditures
    D. Study treatment of existing contingent fee arrangements.
    E. Study tax ramifications involved in merging the two firms and select best alternatives.
    F. Propose billing and collection policies.
    G. Accounting firm
    H. Bank(s)
    I. Propose professional liability coverage and how to handle existing claims.

Exhibit 7
MERGER PRACTICE INTEGRATION SUBCOMMITTEE

I.   Practice management structure

    A. Compare department structure.

       1. Practice areas

       2. Expertise

       3. Practice groups within departments

    B. Compare departmental management.

       1. Department head selection

       2. Department head responsibilities and authority

       3. Practice group leader selection

       4. Practice group leader responsibilities and authority

II. Major clients

    A. Identify types of work performed.

    B. Identify expertise needed.

    C. Identify and study opportunities presented by merger.

III. Quality control systems

    A. Compare case intake procedures.

    B. Propose billing and collection guidelines.

    C. Study work assignment.

    D. Review work supervision.

IV. Organization

    A. Determine whether the firm should be divided into divisions, sections, or departments.

       1. Formality

       2. Practice groups

       3. Functions for each department and, if applicable, practice groups

       4. Role of department heads and, if applicable, practice group leaders

    B. Determine other mechanisms for facilitating communications.

V.   Practice capacity

    A. Identify specialties and subspecialties of each lawyer and paralegal in firm.

    B. Determine how expertise and experience fit with merged firm's practice and staffing requirements.

    C. Identify additional potential requirements that can be forecast.

    D. Develop plan to inform lawyers of the expertise and experience of all lawyers in firm; coordinate with business development and marketing committee.

VI. Practice integration

    A. Identify methods for integrating practices.

    B. Determine how work assignments should be made.

    C. Determine feasibility of staffing projects with lawyers from both firms. If feasible, determine process for best way to get this done.

    D. Define ways to communicate about lawyers' work requirements and time availability.

    E. Determine whether lawyers should be temporarily or permanently transferred between offices on temporary or permanent basis, and if so, how transfers should be accomplished.

    F. Select ways to keep lawyers informed on continuing basis about work being done by other lawyers in firm.

VII. Practice management

    A. Identify methods for monitoring performance of legal services.

    B. Adopt policies for rendering legal opinions, audit letters, preparation of registration statements and other sensitive documents, supervising closings, etc.

    C. Develop systems such as form files, legal memoranda files, etc., to make practice more efficient.

VIII. General information

    A. Determine how integration can best be maintained.

    B. Identify periodic firm functions, including how often and in what forms they should be held, to help integration process.

    C. Consider the need for a permanent integration committee.

Exhibit 8
MERGER CONFLICTS SUBCOMMITTEE

I.   Past cases
II. Current cases
   A. Identify potential conflicts.
   B. Examine referral sources.
   C. Meet with responsible partners to assess significance of conflicts and how they might be resolved.
   D. Propose resolution for handling existing and potential conflicts; coordinate with business development and marketing subcommittee.
III. Ongoing checks
   A. Establish procedures during merger discussions.
   B. Establish procedures for after merger.

Exhibit 9
MERGER RETIREMENT AND BENEFITS SUBCOMMITTEE

Review current benefits and plans and propose benefits and plans for combined firms.

I.   Benefits and perquisites
   A. Health and hospitalization insurance
   B. Life insurance
   C. Disability insurance
   D. Automobile and parking
   E. Business club dues, country clubs, professional associations, bar dues, etc.
   F. Child care
II. Retirement and termination plans and benefits
   A. Pension/profit-sharing plans and other retirement benefits
   B. Death and disability benefits (excluding amounts provided by insurance)
   C. Withdrawal and expulsion payments
   D. Phasedown and early retirement
   E. Mandatory retirement

Exhibit 10
MERGER BUSINESS DEVELOPMENT
AND MARKETING SUBCOMMITTEE

I. Individual marketing efforts
    A. Review each firm's major marketing goals.
    B. Study each firm's specific marketing actions or efforts undertaken and results.
    C. Review each firm's internal marketing structure.
    D. Evaluate the internal marketing resources, such as dedicated marketing staff, used by each firm.
    E. Review the external marketing resources used by each firm (e.g., consultants, public relations firms, graphics specialists, etc.).
    F. Review each firm's budget for marketing expenditures and policies for reimbursement of expenses.
II. Major areas of practice
    A. Review most significant clients for each area.
    B. Evaluate the potential cross-selling opportunities for merged firm.
III. Potential marketing opportunities
    A. Identify merged firm's marketing opportunities.
        1. Marketing efforts to be continued
        2. Marketing efforts to be developed
    B. Determine each firm's current cross-selling and merged firm's efforts.
    C. Identify opportunities for expansion.
        1. New practice areas
        2. New industries
        3. Specific types of clients
IV. Publicity
    A. Develop plan for publicizing merger.
        1. Media coverage
        2. Client notification
        3. Open house
    B. Appoint spokespersons for dealing with media.

    C. Approve merger public relations checklist.

V. Marketing

    A. Develop short-range marketing plan for merged firm; coordinate with practice integration subcommittee.

    B. Identify ways to maximize synergy and interaction among new firm's lawyers; coordinate with practice integration subcommittee.

    C. Work with practice integration subcommittee to develop marketing plan for each practice group/department.

        1. Practice areas that require greatest focus

        2. Industries that require greatest focus

        3. Clients that can be cross-sold immediately

        4. Personal marketing plans for individual lawyers in departments/practice groups

    D. Determine need for production of written marketing materials.

        1. Brochure

        2. Practice area pamphlets

        3. Resumes of individual lawyers

        4. Other

    E. Identify marketing tools to use on firmwide basis.

        1. Speaker's bureau

        2. Membership in civic, social, and trade organizations

        3. Seminars

        4. Client advisories

        5. Newsletters

    F. Develop marketing budget for approval.

Exhibit 11
MERGER ASSOCIATE/PARALEGAL SUBCOMMITTEE

I. Existing personnel
    A. List specialties, abilities, and experience of existing personnel; coordinate with practice integration subcommittee.
    B. List current assignments, compensation, work evaluations, and associates' prospects and eligibility for partnership.
    C. Determine how work assignments for associates and paralegals will be made.
    D. Develop a policy for transferring associates and paralegals among departments and branches of multiple offices.
II. Hiring
    A. Develop policies and guidelines for associate and paralegal recruitment hiring practices.
    B. Identify firm's associate and paralegal needs for coming year; coordinate with practice integration subcommittee.
    C. Decide how recruiting for coming year will be conducted.
        1. Recruiting committee
        2. Law schools
        3. Hiring decisions
        4. Choice of office in multiple-office firm
        5. Summer associate program
    D. Develop policy for hiring lateral associates, credit for clerkships and other experience.
III. Compensation
    A. Determine starting salary for new associates.
    B. If multiple offices, determine if there should be a dual compensation plan for each office.
    C. Determine whether firm pays one-time bonuses to new associates, moving expenses, bar examination course fees, bar dues, etc.
    D. Develop a compensation plan.
        1. Straight salary, bonuses or other incentive plans
        2. Lockstep-seniority or individual merit

  3. Compensation and fringe benefits vs. direct compensation
  4. Compensation of existing associates/paralegals
  5. Cost of integrating the two compensation systems
IV. Training and evaluation
  A. Adopt program for training and supervising associates and paralegals.
  B. Agree on evaluation system for associates and paralegals.
    1. How often and in what form
    2. Evaluation standards
    3. Eligibility for partnership
    4. Associates and paralegals having difficulty
    5. Termination of associates and paralegals
V. Partnership
  A. Determine how to handle associates who have been assured partnership.
  B. Agree on partnership track for combined firm and how associates will be slotted.
  C. Agree on other partnership criteria.
  D. Agree on decision-making process for admitting new partners.
  E. Determine whether any associates will experience a change in status, i.e., become a permanent associate, a staff attorney.
VI. General
  A. Determine whether there should be a permanent associate/paralegal committee.
  B. Develop policies to enhance associate and paralegal communication, as well as integration of associates and paralegals; coordinate with practice integration subcommittee.

Exhibit 12
PARTNER COMPENSATION SYSTEM COMPARISON

	Firm A	Firm B
Decision-making body		
Method of selection of decision makers		
Term of office		
Type of compensation system		
Compensation philosophy		
Compensation process		
Timing of compensation decisions		
Factors considered		
Movement within system (up or down)		
Description of bonus system		
Range of compensation		
Draw approach		

Exhibit 13
MANAGEMENT SYSTEM COMPARISON

	Firm A	Firm B
Governing body		
Method of selection		
Size of group		
Term of office		
Authority/responsibility		
Voting requirements		
Culture/style		
Office governing structure		
Practice management structure		

Exhibit 14
PRACTICE MANAGEMENT STRUCTURE COMPARISON

	Firm A	Firm B
List of departments/sections		
Size		
List of practice groups within departments/sections		
Size		
Functions performed by department		
Work assignment		
Case intake guidelines		
Billing and collection policies and procedures		
Describe department management		
Describe selection of department heads		
Describe role and responsibilities of department heads		
Describe practice group management		
Describe selection of practice group leaders		
Describe role and responsibilities of practice group leaders		

Exhibit 15
INFORMATION REQUIRED FOR MERGER ANALYSIS

With respect to the following, analyze information for each firm's last three complete accounting years, plus year-to-date results for the current year (as applicable):

Income Statement/Cash Flows

A. Detailed profit/loss statements (at year-end and year-to-date) and detailed operating budget for current year.

B. Schedule of extraordinary fees received (e.g., large contingency settlement or fees in excess of time recorded) or expenses incurred (e.g., moving costs, leasehold, or capital expenditures) during the period.

C. Weighted census of full-time equivalent separated into the following categories (as applicable), by year. If possible, include the census that the current year's operating budget is based on, as well as the year-to-date statistics.

   ◆ Equity owners (partners/shareholders)
   ◆ Non-equity owner (special tier of non-equity lawyers held out as owners)
   ◆ Current equity owners with special compensation arrangements (including retiring partners and others with special compensation arrangements)
   ◆ Retired owners or others who receive income from the firm
   ◆ Contract lawyers (part-time or special compensation arrangements)
   ◆ Associates (employed lawyers)
   ◆ Students
   ◆ Paralegals/legal assistants
   ◆ Law clerks
   ◆ Secretaries
   ◆ Support staff subject to outsourcing arrangements
   ◆ Senior administrative staff (by position)
   ◆ Other support staff

Weighted census means, for example, that if an associate was elevated to partner on the first day of the third month in the firm's accounting year, that lawyer would be included as $^2/_{12}$ or .17 of an associate and $^{10}/_{12}$ or .83 of a partner for that year. *Be sure to include in the census all personnel, including those who have departed during the relative time period as well as those still with the firm.*

D. Schedule of billable/nonbillable hours, write-offs, and billings for all timekeepers (sorted and subtotaled by timekeeper type) for each period.

E. Value of time worked (billable hours multiplied by standard billing rates in effect during period, sorted and subtotaled by timekeeper type), and fees billed and collected, by period.

F. Billing rates for all timekeepers and effective dates.

G. For each year, a list of top 50 clients based on fees received (sorted high to low, if possible).

H. List of clients and fees by responsible lawyer (not required during initial analysis).

I. List of clients and fees by practice area (not required during initial analysis).

J. For each year, a schedule of owner compensation, as shown on attached Worksheet Number One. With respect to the "other" category, include payments for automobile expenses, country club dues, payroll taxes on behalf of shareholders, life and disability insurance premiums, etc. Indicate period covered by compensation. For professional corporations, indicate the dollar value of bonuses paid and year of payment.

K. For each year, a schedule of compensation paid to all other lawyers, organized as shown on Worksheet Number Two.

Balance Sheet

L. For each year-end and year-to-date, detailed balance sheets.

M. For each year-end and year-to-date, aged summaries of work in process and accounts receivable, separating fees and client costs. Indicate total amount of contingencies.

N. Current, detailed capital budgets (budgeted changes in fixed assets, debt, capitalization, etc.).

O. Schedule of permanent partner/shareholder capital.

P. Schedule of liabilities (describe) for, and payments to, former, deceased, or retired partners/shareholders.

Other

Q. Copies of firm operating agreements, including the current partnership/shareholder agreement and any other agreements affecting the operations of the firm.

R. List and explanation of pending lawsuits against the firm.

Owner Compensation

Worksheet Number One

Owner Name	% Share of Net Income	Base Draw	Additional Distributions	Pension or Profit Sharing Contribution	Other	Total

Compensation of All Other Lawyers
Worksheet Number Two

Lawyer Name	Position	Base Salary	Bonus	Other	Total

Exhibit 16
PRO FORMA MEETING AGENDA

I.   General Assumptions
    A. Effective date
    B. Fiscal year
    C. Administrative structure
    D. Method of combination
    E. Partnership admission
    F. Staff lawyers, senior lawyers, two-tier partnership
    G. Partner draws, method

II. Revenue Assumptions
    A. Extraordinary/contingency fees
    B. Average billable hours
    C. Billing rate changes
    D. Realization
    E. Billing and collection cycle
        1. Hiring plans
        2. Lawyers
        3. Legal assistants
        4. Summer clerks
    F. Known conflicts that will result in loss of business
    G. Anticipated loss of referral work
    H. Projected lost time for integration

III. Expense Assumptions
    A. Administration: hiring, elimination of positions, salary increases, bonus plan
    B. Location of accounting function
    C. Associate compensation: starting salary, salary increases, signing bonus, other bonus
    D. Legal assistant compensation
    E. Summer clerk compensation
    F. Cost (savings) of employee benefits integration
    G. Pension plan costs
    H. Office automation
        1. Equipment

2. Software
3. Personnel
4. Conversion costs
5. Projected savings
I. Professional liability insurance
J. Office space costs, design, build outs
K. Office moving costs
L. Lawyer relocation
M. Recruiting costs
N. Employment fees
O. Library costs (savings)
P. Firm meetings and travel
Q. Interoffice freight
R. Communications
S. Professional fees and services
T. Announcements, stationery, office supplies
U. Brochure, newsletter, other publications
V. Donations and contributions
W. Interest expense
   1. Partner draws
   2. Additional capital expenditures
X. Retired partner costs

Exhibits 17–19
PRO FORMA SCHEDULES

Introduction

To assist the partners in assessing the financial implications of a merger, the following three exhibits should be prepared to show the combined financial projection for the merged firm during the first three years of operations. These exhibits are interrelated; some adjustments may affect more than one statement. In preparing these statements for a prospective merger, adopt a principle of conservatism, which results in anticipating all possible expenses while realistically assessing the increase in revenue resulting from practice synergy.

These projections should be included as part of the material circulated to all partners to assist them in making their decision on the merger. These projections should not be regarded as an operating budget for the combined firm. Instead, they should be viewed as the merger committee's best estimate of the merged firm's performance during the first three years. Once the merger has taken place, a detailed operating budget should be prepared under the direction of the merged firm's executive committee.

Exhibit 17

Cash Basis Income Statement Analysis

	Calendar/Fiscal Year Budgeted			Combined Firm Calendar/Fiscal Year Adjusted Budget	Merged Firm Projection	Merged Firm Projection	Merged Firm Projection
	Firm A	Firm B	Merger-Related Costs/(Savings)	Firm Name	Firm Name Merger Year +1	Firm Name Merger Year +2	Firm Name Merger Year +3
Revenues:							
Fee income	$ —	$ —	$ —	$ —	$ —	$ —	$ —
Contingent fee income	—	—	—	—	—	—	—
Interest & other income	—	—	—	—	—	—	—
Total Revenue	$ —	$ —	$ —	$ —	$ —	$ —	$ —
Per Lawyer	—	—	—	—	—	—	—
Expenses:							
Employee Costs							
Legal:							
Lawyer compensation	$ —	$ —	$ —	$ —	$ —	$ —	$ —
Non-lawyer legal staff salaries	—	—	—	—	—	—	—
Total legal staff salaries & bonuses	$ —	$ —	$ —	$ —	$ —	$ —	$ —
Administrative:							
Secretary & word processing salaries	$ —	$ —	$ —	$ —	$ —	$ —	$ —
Other administrative staff salaries	—	—	—	—	—	—	—
Total administrative staff salaries & bonuses	$ —	$ —	$ —	$ —	$ —	$ —	$ —
Salary & Bonus Summary:							
Total legal & administrative salaries	$ —	$ —	$ —	$ —	$ —	$ —	$ —
Total legal & administrative bonuses	—	—	—	—	—	—	—
Total Legal & Administrative Salary & Bonuses	$ —	$ —	$ —	$ —	$ —	$ —	$ —
Per Lawyer	—	—	—	—	—	—	—

Other Employee Costs
- Mandatory employee benefits — $ ____
- Discretionary employee benefits — $ ____
- Lateral hire recruiting — $ ____
- Merger-related relocations — $ ____
- Temp. employee & other costs — $ ____
  - Total Other Employee Costs — $ ____

Total Employee Costs — $ ____
Per Lawyer — $ ____

Occupancy Costs
- Rent (incl. operating expense/escalation) — $ ____
- Maintenance, repairs & amortization — $ ____
- Utilities & other occupancy — $ ____

Occupancy Costs — $ ____
Per Lawyer — $ ____

Professional Costs — $ ____
Per Lawyer — $ ____

Outside Services — $ ____
Per Lawyer — $ ____

Office Operating Expense
- Office copier expenses — $ ____
- Depreciation & amortization
- Printing, stationery & supplies
- Computer supplies & software
  - Achieve technological parity
- Publications & services
- Equipment rental, maintenance & repairs
- Communication expenses
- Miscellaneous expenses
- Library expense
- Service chargebacks
- Post-merger integration/travel

Office Operating Expense — $ ____
Per Lawyer

Exhibit 17
Cash Basis Income Statement Analysis (continued)

	Calendar/Fiscal Year Budgeted		Merger-Related Costs/(Savings)	Combined Firm Calendar/Fiscal Year Adjusted Budget	Merged Firm Projection	Merged Firm Projection	Merged Firm Projection
	Firm A	Firm B		Firm Name	Firm Name Merger Year +1	Firm Name Merger Year +2	Firm Name Merger Year +3
Insurance Expense							
Errors & omissions	$ —	$ —	$ —	$ —	$ —	$ —	$ —
General insurance	—	—	—	—	—	—	—
Insurance Expense	$ —	$ —	$ —	$ —	$ —	$ —	$ —
Per Lawyer	—	—		—	—	—	—
Interest Expense	$ —	$ —	$ —	$ —	$ —	$ —	$ —
Per Lawyer	—	—		—	—	—	—
Business & Property Taxes	$ —	$ —	$ —	$ —	$ —	$ —	$ —
Per Lawyer	—	—		—	—	—	—
Bad Debt Expense	$ —	$ —	$ —	$ —	$ —	$ —	$ —
Per Lawyer	—	—		—	—	—	—
Payments to Former Partners/Employees							
Payments to former partners	$ —	$ —	$ —	$ —	$ —	$ —	$ —
Payments to former employees	—	—	—	—	—	—	—
Payments to Former Partners/Employees	$ —	$ —	$ —	$ —	$ —	$ —	$ —
Per Lawyer	—	—		—	—	—	—
Total Expenses	—	—		—	—	—	—
Expenses Per Lawyer							
Net Income Available to Partners	—			—	—	—	—
Per Equity Partner							

Exhibit 18
Cash Flow Statement

Firm Name
Statement of Cash Flows
Budgeted Calendar/Fiscal Year
(in thousands of dollars)

	Month 1	Month 2	Month 3	Month 4	Month 5	Month 6	Month 7	Month 8	Month 9	Month 10	Month 11	Month 12
CASH BALANCE AT BEGINNING OF PERIOD PER BOOKS	$ —	$ —	$ —	$ —	$ —	$ —	$ —	$ —	$ —	$ —	$ —	$ —
Cash flow from Operating Activity:												
Net income	—	—	—	—	—	—	—	—	—	—	—	—
Adjustments to net income												
Depreciation & amortization	—	—	—	—	—	—	—	—	—	—	—	—
Client disbursement write-offs	—	—	—	—	—	—	—	—	—	—	—	—
Increase/(decrease) in unapplied cash	—	—	—	—	—	—	—	—	—	—	—	—
Increase/(decrease) in bonus accruals	—	—	—	—	—	—	—	—	—	—	—	—
Increase/(decrease) in E&O accruals	—	—	—	—	—	—	—	—	—	—	—	—
Increase in other liabilities	—	—	—	—	—	—	—	—	—	—	—	—
Total Adjustments	—	—	—	—	—	—	—	—	—	—	—	—
Cash Provided by Operating Activities	—	—	—	—	—	—	—	—	—	—	—	—
Cash Flow from Investing Activities:												
Property & equipment expenditures	—	—	—	—	—	—	—	—	—	—	—	—
Other Cash Adjustments:												
Dist. draws & bonus to income partners	—	—	—	—	—	—	—	—	—	—	—	—
Guaranteed payments to former partners	—	—	—	—	—	—	—	—	—	—	—	—
Partner carryover cash distributions	—	—	—	—	—	—	—	—	—	—	—	—
Payment of permanent capital to departed partners	—	—	—	—	—	—	—	—	—	—	—	—
Payment of permanent capital to overfunded partners	—	—	—	—	—	—	—	—	—	—	—	—
Contributions to capital	—	—	—	—	—	—	—	—	—	—	—	—
Repayment of term loans	—	—	—	—	—	—	—	—	—	—	—	—
Other cash distributions/collections	—	—	—	—	—	—	—	—	—	—	—	—
Total Cash Adjustments	—	—	—	—	—	—	—	—	—	—	—	—
Net Increase/(Decrease) in Cash	—	—	—	—	—	—	—	—	—	—	—	—
Cash Balance at End of Period per Books	—	—	—	—	—	—	—	—	—	—	—	—
Float (Checks written, but not cashed)	—	—	—	—	—	—	—	—	—	—	—	—
Cash Balance at End of Period per Bank	—	—	—	—	—	—	—	—	—	—	—	—

Note: This schedule should be prepared for each firm based on their respective budgets (pre-merger), the combined firm during the year the merger takes place, and the merged firm during its first three years of operation.

Exhibit 19
Economic Balance Sheet

	Firm A			Firm B			Merged Firm (Firm A + Firm B)		
	Cash Basis Balance Sheet	Adjustments	Economic Balance	Cash Basis Balance Sheet	Adjustments	Economic Balance	Cash Basis Balance Sheet	Adjustments	Economic Balance
Assets									
Cash & cash equivalents	$ —	$ —	$ —	$ —	$ —	$ —	$ —	$ —	$ —
Marketable securities	—	—	—	—	—	—	—	—	—
Client trust funds	—	—	—	—	—	—	—	—	—
Client disbursement receivables	—	(1)	—	—	(1)	—	—	(1)	—
A/R—partners & employees	—	—	—	—	—	—	—	—	—
Prepaid expenses	—	—	—	—	—	—	—	—	—
Other current assets	—	—	—	—	—	—	—	—	—
Fixed assets (net of depreciation)	—	—	—	—	—	—	—	—	—
Other non-current assets	—	(2)	—	—	(2)	—	—	(2)	—
Work in process (less reserves)	—	(3)	—	—	(3)	—	—	(3)	—
Accounts receivable (less reserves)	—	—	—	—	—	—	—	—	—
Total Assets	$ —	$ —	$ —	$ —	$ —	$ —	$ —	$ —	$ —
Liabilities									
Line of credit	$ —	$ —	$ —	$ —	$ —	$ —	$ —	$ —	$ —
Current portion of long-term debt	—	—	—	—	—	—	—	—	—
Pension/profit sharing payable	—	—	—	—	—	—	—	—	—
Payroll withholdings	—	—	—	—	—	—	—	—	—
Client trust funds	—	—	—	—	—	—	—	—	—
Interest payable	—	—	—	—	—	—	—	—	—
Other current liabilities	—	—	—	—	—	—	—	—	—
Long-term debt	—	—	—	—	—	—	—	—	—
Other non-current liabilities	—	(4)	—	—	(4)	—	—	(4)	—
Unfunded retirement plans	—	—	—	—	—	—	—	—	—
Total Liabilities	$ —	$ —	$ —	$ —	$ —	$ —	$ —	$ —	$ —

Capital

Contributed capital	$ ——		$ ——		$ ——		$ ——		$ ——
Undistributed earnings	——		——		——		——		——
Economic capital	——		——		——		——		——
Total Capital	$ ——		$ ——		$ ——		$ ——		$ ——
Total Liabilities and Capital	$ ——		$ ——		$ ——		$ ——		$ ——

Key Ratios

Assets per equity partner	$ ——		$ ——		$ ——		$ ——		$ ——
Liabilities per equity partner	$ ——		$ ——		$ ——		$ ——		$ ——
Debt per equity partner	$ ——		$ ——		$ ——		$ ——		$ ——
Contributed capital per equity partner	$ ——		$ ——		$ ——		$ ——		$ ——
Capital per equity partner	$ ——		$ ——		$ ——		$ ——		$ ——

NOTES: Accrual adjustments may include:

1. Adjusted to realizable value based on firm's historical realization percentage.
2. Based on outstanding work in process at end of period, adjusted for estimated billing and collection realization rates.
3. Based on outstanding fees receivable at end of period, adjusted for estimated collection realization rate.
4. Estimated present value of the firm's unfunded retirement plan.

Exhibit 20
MERGER PROSPECTUS TABLE OF CONTENTS

I. Executive Summary
II. Merger Committee Report and Recommendations
   A. Background Information
      1. Brief Firm Histories
         a. Firm A
         b. Firm B
      2. Strategic Objectives of the Constituent Firms
   B. Committee Comments and Observations
      1. Firm Cultures
      2. Practice Considerations
      3. Synergy
         a. Practice Area A, B, C, etc.
      4. Strategic Initiatives
      5. Financial Considerations
      6. Absence of Material Conflicts
      7. Conclusions and Recommendations
III. New Firm Structure and Governance
   A. Name of Firm
   B. Effective Date
   C. Legal Entity
   D. Transitional Year Financial Arrangement (if necessary)
   E. Initial Governance Structure
      1. Organizational Functions
   F. Partnership Structure and Voting Requirements
   G. Equity Partner Compensation
   H. Capital
   I. Partner Retirement
   J. Associates
   K. New Partnership Agreement
IV. Financial Comparisons, Projection Assumptions, and Consolidation Issues
   A. Introduction
   B. Comparison of Financial Performance

1. Noteworthy Items and Trends
2. Revenue
3. Expenses
4. Net Income
5. Leverage Ratios
6. Billable Hours Comparison
7. Billing Rate Comparison
8. Inventory and Realization Comparison
9. Balance Sheet Comparison
10. Top Client Analysis

V. Development of Pro Forma Income Statements
    A. Introduction
    B. General Comments on Revenue and Expense Assumptions
    C. Pro Forma Assumptions

VI. Economic Balance Sheet

VII. Statement of Cash Flows

VIII. Transition Year Income Allocation (if necessary)

IX. Allocation of Fees Generated from Contingency Fee Matters

X. Index of Appendices
    A. Side-by-Side Financial Profiles
    B. Pro Forma Projections
    C. Cash Flow Projections
    D. Economic Balance Sheet
    E. Tax Opinion (if necessary)
    F. Comparison of Key Obligations

Exhibit 21
SAMPLE MERGER TERM SHEET

Memorandum of Agreement for the Merger of ABC and XYZ

1. *Name.* The name of the merged firm will be ABXY.

2. *Effective Date.* The effective date of the merger will be January 1, 20__.

3. *Articles of Partnership.* The Articles of Partnership of the merged firm will be based on the Articles of Partnership of ABC, with such changes as may be necessary to give effect to the terms of the merger. On the effective date, the partners of XYZ will be admitted as equity partners of ABC, and the partnership name will be changed to ABXY.

4. *Executive Committee.* The Executive Committee for the merged firm will consist of two members designated by ABC and one member designated by XYZ. The term of the XYZ designee will be three years; the terms of ABC designees will be one and two years. Thereafter all vacancies on the Executive Committee will be filled without regard to the member's prior firm. Future terms will be three years, and members may be elected for an unlimited number of terms.

5. *Managing Partner.* The Managing Partner will be elected by the Executive Committee from its members.

6. *Other Committees.* The Executive Committee of the merged firm will determine the need for committees and will appoint all committees.

7. *Decisions Reserved to Partners.* The Executive Committee will have responsibility to handle all business affairs of the firm, with full authority to make all decisions not specifically reserved to the partners. The following decisions are reserved to the partners:

- Admission or expulsion of partners (special majority).
- Change of firm name (special majority).
- Dissolution of the firm (special majority).
- Establishment of the firm's line of credit.

+ Approval of all expenditures in excess of $100,000 not provided for in the firm's budget.
+ Election of the Executive Committee.
+ All matters relating to death, disability, retirement, voluntary withdrawal, and expulsion (special majority).
+ Merger.
+ Opening branch offices.
+ Change in the compensation system.
+ Change in the firm's capital structure.

8. *Voting Percentages.* Voting will be based on percentage of profits. Special majority means 75 percent.

9. *Compensation.* The compensation process of ABC will be implemented, subject to the transition period described below. On the effective date, the equity partners of the merged firm will be assigned income percentages that will remain in effect for twelve months as follows: The ABC equity partners as a group will receive 60 percent of the income percentages of the merged firm, and the Executive Committee will allocate the income among the ABC equity partners, subject to approval of the ABC partners. The XYZ equity partners as a group will receive 40 percent of the income percentages of the merged firm, which the Executive Committee will allocate among the XYZ partners, subject to the approval of the XYZ partners. In allocating percentages, the Executive Committee of the merged firm will act with a view to establishing a fair and equitable allocation of income percentages throughout the firm.

Effective January 1, 20__, the merged firm will adjust income percentages without regard to the partner's prior firm. Compensation will be based on a partner's contribution to the merged firm as a whole. Compensation will be set by the Executive Committee.

10. *Partners' Draws.* The equity partners of the merged firm will receive monthly draws against their anticipated net earnings from the partnership in amounts determined from time to time by the Executive Committee. The total monthly draw will be allocated pro rata among the equity partners in accordance with income percentages. Supplemental distributions to partners may be

declared from time to time by the Executive Committee if the firm's cash position permits.

11. *Partners' Capital Accounts.* Total partnership capital for the merged firm will be $500,000. Each partner will be required to maintain a capital account balance based on his/her income percentage. For example, a partner whose income percentage is 3 percent will be required to make a capital contribution of $15,000. Attachment __ (not shown) shows the capital position of each partner as of the effective date of the merger.

Partners who have a negative capital balance will be required to contribute additional capital within three months of the effective date of merger. If a partner wishes to finance the capital contribution, the merged firm will guarantee repayment of the loan provided the loan is amortized over five or fewer years. Partners whose capital position is above the required amount will be reimbursed in accordance with terms to be developed by the Executive Committee.

12. *Work in Progress and Accounts Receivable.* Each firm's accounts receivable and work in progress will be contributed to the combined firm.

13. *Tenure to Partnership.* The merged firm will consider associates for election to salaried partnership effective January 1 of each year. Except in unusual circumstances, an associate must have completed approximately eight years with the firm to be eligible for election to partnership. Normally, associates will be elected to salaried partnership. Existing XYZ policies and criteria with respect to admission of associates to salaried or equity partnership and admission of salaried partners to equity partnership will apply to the merged firm.

14. *Nepotism.* The XYZ antinepotism policy will apply to the merged firm; however, exceptions to this policy now existing among ABC personnel will be grandfathered.

15. *Income from Law-Related Sources.* The ABC policy that income from law-related sources such as director's fees, teaching salaries, etc., is paid into the firm will apply to the merged firm.

16. *Deferred Compensation.* The XYZ partners' retirement plan will be rolled over into the ABC partners' retirement plan, and the

XYZ partners will become participants in and contributors to the ABC plan on the same basis as ABC partners. Benefits for death, disability, withdrawal, and expulsion will be those currently provided to the ABC partners.

17. *Associate Compensation.* The Executive Committee will adjust associate salaries as of the effective date of the merger, as appropriate based on an analysis of market. Thereafter, associate compensation will be set annually, effective January 1.

18. *Staff Compensation and Benefits.* ABC personnel policies with respect to staff compensation, benefits, and other matters will apply to the merged firm. The merged firm will in good faith address any inequity that this may cause to XYZ personnel.

19. *Administrative Systems and Equipment.* On the effective date, all XYZ timekeeping personnel will be added to the ABC timekeeping system. The administrative systems and office equipment used by the merged firm will be determined by the Administrator, subject to review by the Executive Committee.

20. *Practice Management.* Prior to the effective date or as soon thereafter as practicable, the Executive Committee of the merged firm will implement an integrated practice management structure.

21. *Partnership Approval.* This agreement is subject to approval by the requisite vote of the ABC partnership and the XYZ partnership.

Dated this _____ day of _____, 20_____.

Exhibit 22
PUBLIC RELATIONS CHECKLIST

I. Preliminary measures
   A. If media consultant will be used, notify as early as possible, well before scheduled announcement date.
   B. Draw up contingency plan in case word leaks out (as it often does).
   C. Swear all parties to secrecy.
   D. Choose information contact persons.
      1. One for each firm
      2. One for each branch office (vis-à-vis local media)
      3. Backups for each
   E. Schedule plan.
      1. Date for notification of key clients
      2. Date for notification of all clients
      3. Dates for notification of all partners, associates, and staff
      4. Date for press release
   F. Prepare fact sheet and approve contents.
   G. Prepare press release(s) and have approved.
   H. Prepare information package.
      1. Contents
         a. Fact sheet
         b. Press release
         c. Firm brochures and other promotional material
         d. Published articles about the firms
      2. Distribution
         a. Clients, press, firm members, others
II. Informing clients
   A. Prepare for client contacts.
      1. Benefits to clients
      2. Client concerns and questions, answers
   B. Prepare for meetings with clients.
      1. Who
      2. When

       3. Appointments

       4. Contact attorneys

       5. Need for confidentiality

  C. Call clients.

       1. Who

       2. When

       3. Contact attorney

       4. Need for confidentiality

  D. Prepare letters to clients.

       1. Mailing list

       2. Date of mailing

       3. Text

          a. Content

             i. Benefits to clients

             ii. Client concerns to address or to be addressed.

          b. Multiple versions

             i. Each firm

             ii. Different types of clients

       4. Approval

       5. Signature (managing partner, billing partner, or responsible lawyer)

       6. Information on other firm (brochure, published articles, etc.) and/or fact sheet and/or press release

III. Informing the press

  A. Prepare a plan for contacting press.

       1. Simultaneous release or other approach

       2. Media to contact personally and by whom: national general press, national business press, national legal press, local general media, local business press, relevant trade publications (vis-à-vis practice specialties)

       3. Possible press questions

       4. Answers for possible press questions

  B. Prepare press list for blanket distribution of press release.

IV. Internal communications

  A. Prepare memo to lawyers and staff.

       1. Official spokespersons

       2. Official information they can divulge if asked

    B. Determine if any meetings are necessary.

V. Projects to consider

    A. Plan press conference.

        1. Lawyers preparation

        2. Date and place

        3. Plan for contacting media

    B. Plan social events (open houses, seminars, etc., to introduce clients to new partners).

    C. Prepare tombstone ads.

        1. Text

        2. Publications in which they will appear

        3. Typesetting

VI. Follow-up

    A. Have new letterhead designed, approved, and printed.

    B. Make formal announcement.

        1. Text

        2. Mailing list

        3. Design and production

    C. Make announcement in firm newsletter(s).

    D. Print brochure and other materials.

    E. Notify *American Lawyer, National Law Journal,* and other trade publications that run annual surveys listing law firms by size.

Exhibit 23
FACT SHEET

I. Existing firm (one for each firm)
    A. Main contact person for press
    B. Backup contact
    C. Contacts for branch offices (with backups)
    D. Office location (address and telephone number)
    E. Number of partners, associates, paralegals, and staff
    F. Relative size of firm in a relevant geographical area (e.g., "the __th largest firm in city, state, region, nation")
    G. Characterization of firm (e.g., "a full-service firm with specialties or concentrations in telecommunications, antitrust and trade regulation, and tax")
    H. Other substantial practice areas not mentioned as specialties above
    I. Notable lawyers in firm (e.g., former high city, state, or federal officials in the executive, legislative, or judicial branches; current or former high officials of significant legal or trade associations; board members of significant corporations; and others who might interest the press)
    J. Major clients who would not object to being listed
    K. Names in any mergers over past five years, number of lawyers in each, when it took place, etc.
    L. Notable accomplishments (e.g., major cases or transactions)
    M. Other relevant information of potential interest
II. New firm
    (If information has already been provided in part I above, merge information provided by both firms and be prepared to eliminate some of it. Also, indicate which information cannot be distributed universally.)
    A. Name
    B. Reason for merger
    C. Number of partners, associates, paralegals, and staff
    D. Office that will be dropped or added

E. Any changes in location of either firm or any branch offices

F. Relative size of firm (e.g., "will make the firm the nation's __th largest in city, state, region, nation").

G. Characterization (e.g., "a full-service firm specializing in . . .")

H. Major practice areas not mentioned above (in approximate order of importance)

I. Plans for further expansion

J. Other significant changes

K. Date of merger vote

L. Date merger becomes effective

M. Management structure

N. Key management members and their positions

O. Lawyers who will be leaving and why

P. Lawyers making or losing partnership

Q. Lawyers who will be transferred to other offices

R. Notable lawyers (merge individual firm responses)

S. Firm's major target client types (e.g., large corporations, high-tech firms, investment banking firms, health-care providers)

T. Major clients who would not object to being listed (merge individual firm responses)

U. Clients that firm will lose as a result of merger and why

Exhibit 24
TYPICAL PRESS QUESTIONS

1. Why are the firms merging?
2. Isn't this really an acquisition?
3. Was either firm in any financial or other difficulty?
4. Who suggested merger first?
5. How did the discussions come about?
6. Where will the firm be based?
7. Will the firm drop or add any offices?
8. Will any lawyers be leaving either firm? If so, why?
9. Will all current partners remain partners?
10. Will any lawyers be transferred to other offices?
11. Do the firms have different tracks to partnership? If so, how will differences be resolved?
12. Who will run the new firm?
13. What will the management structure be?
14. Have or will any clients be dropped for conflict reasons?
15. Are any clients leaving either firm as a result of the merger?
16. Are there any plans for further expansion?
17. What kinds of clients will the new firm be targeting?
18. What are annual billings for each firm?
19. What are anticipated billings for the merged firm?
20. How was the name chosen?
21. What were contentious issues during negotiations?
22. Have they all been resolved?
23. Has either firm had any significant defections recently? If so, was that a factor in the merger?
    (Determine any controversial or confidential issues in either firm, and depending on the likelihood of their becoming public knowledge, prepare responses.)

Exhibit 25
MERGER DISCUSSION AGENDA FOR THE ADMINISTRATORS

I. General
   A. Draft a sample organization chart.
   B. Compile a list of new positions needed.
   C. Provide job descriptions for all new positions to be added.
   D. Identify duplicate positions; include a timetable for eliminating positions.
   E. Draft a memorandum on integrating more than one office (space considerations, administrative support, communications and equipment integration, timetable, etc.).

II. Personnel
   A. Compare approaches and philosophy to recruiting, screening, hiring, evaluating, and terminating staff.
   B. Compare systems of personnel use and supervision.
   C. Compare pay differences between branch offices and between firms.
   D. Draft policies on the following:
      1. Vacation
      2. Illness
      3. Holidays
      4. Maternity/paternity
      5. Part-time workers
      6. Overtime
      7. Staff promotion and personal development
      8. Other firm issues (smoking, dress code, etc.)
   E. Discuss participation in lawyer recruiting (list law schools contacted, arrangements made for screening resumes and setting up interviews, summer intern program, etc.).
   F. Compile lists of documents and orientation provided to new associates and new partners.
   G. Compare benefits packages for the following and note any variances between branches:
      1. Paid leaves of absence/sabbaticals

    2. Disability benefits

    3. Health insurance

    4. Death benefit

    5. Retirement plans

    6. Child care

    7. Parking, dues, meals, and other employee benefits provided

III. Economics

    A. Discuss types and uses of management reports each firm provides.

    B. Describe timekeeping, billing, and collection procedures. Note problem areas.

    C. Discuss how delinquent accounts, write-offs, and write-downs are handled.

    D. Discuss philosophy of determining debt and capital levels.

    E. Discuss each firm's banking and accounting relationships and any special ties (nepotism, significant business referrals, etc.).

    F. Discuss assumptions used in long-range planning and for recommending billing rate increases.

IV. Facilities

    A. Compile a list of equipment and space commitments, leases, service contracts, etc.

    B. Discuss policy and arrangement for storage and disposal of firm documents and files.

    C. Compare security and maintenance arrangements.

V. Technology

    A. Assess overall needs of merged firm.

    B. Determine whether existing systems can be used, integrated, and at what cost.

        1. Telephone systems

        2. Internal communications

        3. Computer systems

        4. Library and information systems

    C. Estimate conversion costs for documents.

    D. Estimate training costs and procedures.

VI. Systems, procedures, and services
  A. Compare staff, lawyer, and other office policy and procedure manuals.
  B. Compare CLE policies and programs.
  C. List standard forms, indexes, library materials, computer services, etc., that increase lawyer productivity.
  D. Discuss how to handle interoffice communication.
VII. Insurance
VIII. Compare coverage for the following policies:
  A. Accidents and travel
  B. Casualty
  C. Professional liability
  D. Bonding
  E. Other risk reduction

Index

Compensation Plans for Law Firms, Fourth Edition

Edited by James D. Cotterman, Altman Weil, Inc.
Discover how to align your firm's compensation plans with your culture, business objectives, and market realities and find complete and systematic guidance on how to establish workable plans for compensating partners and associates, as well as other contributors to the firm. The book features valuable data from leading legal consulting firm Altman Weil's surveys on law firm performance and compensation, retirement and withdrawal systems. You'll see where your firm stands on salaries and bonuses, as well as detailed analyses of compensation plans for everyone in your firm.

The Essential Formbook: Comprehensive Management Tools for Lawyers

By Gary A. Munneke and Anthony E. Davis
Volume I: Partnership and Organizational Agreements/ Client Intake and Fee Agreements
Volume II: Human Resources/Fees, Billing, and Collection
Volume III: Calendar Docket and File Management/Law Firm Financial Analysis
Useful to legal practitioners of all specialties and sizes, these volumes will help you establish profitable, affirmative client relationships so you can avoid unnecessary risks associated with malpractice and disciplinary complaints. And, with all the forms available on CD-ROM, it's easy to modify them to match your specific needs.

Law Office Policy & Procedures Manual, 2004 Fourth Edition

By Robert C. Wert and Howard I. Hatoff
Now updated with all previous supplements, the 2004 fourth edition includes everything you need to create a complete, customized manual that can serve as a reference guide for current staff and a training tool for new employees, associates, and temp workers. Using the accompanying CD-ROM, you can edit text to produce your own firm's manual and revise it in the future. This concise manual provides everything you need to set policies and establish procedures that will keep your office operating efficiently and productively.

The Lawyer's Guide to Extranets: Breaking Down Walls, Building Client Connections

by Douglas Simpson and Mark Tamminga
An extranet can be a powerful tool that allows law firms to exchange information and build relationships with clients. This new book shows you why extranets are the next step in client interaction and communications, and how you can effectively implement an extranet in any type of firm. This book will take you step-by step through the issues of implementing an extranet, and how to plan and build one. You'll get real-world extranet case studies, and learn from the successes and failures of those who have gone before. Help your firm get ahead of the emerging technologies curve and discover the benefits of adopting this new information tool.

The Lawyer's Guide to Fact Finding on the Internet, Second Edition

By Carole A. Levitt and Mark E. Rosch
Written especially for legal professionals, this revised and expanded edition is a complete hands-on guide to the best sites, secrets, and shortcuts for conducting efficient research on the Web. Containing over 600 pages of information, with over 100 screen shots of specific Web sites, this resource is filled with practical tips and advice on using specific sites, alerting readers to quirks or hard-to-find information. What's more, user-friendly icons immediately identify free sites, free-with-registration sites, and pay sites. An accompanying CD-ROM includes the links contained in the book, indexed, so you can easily navigate to these cream-of-the-crop Web sites without typing URLs into your browser. Also, be sure to subscribe to *The Lawyer's Guide to Fact Finding on the Internet E-mail Newsletter* to stay current on the most valuable Web sites!

LAW PRACTICE MANAGEMENT SECTION
MARKETING • MANAGEMENT • TECHNOLOGY • FINANCE

The Lawyer's Guide to Marketing Your Practice, Second Edition

Edited by James A. Durham and Deborah McMurray

This book is packed with practical ideas, innovative strategies, useful checklists, and sample marketing and action plans to help you implement a successful, multi-faceted, and profit-enhancing marketing plan for your firm. Organized into four sections, this illuminating resource covers: Developing Your Approach; Enhancing Your Image; Implementing Marketing Strategies and Maintaining Your Program. Appendix materials include an instructive primer on market research to inform you on research methodologies that support the marketing of legal services. The accompanying CD-ROM contains a wealth of checklists, plans, and other sample reports, questionnaires, and templates—all designed to make implementing your marketing strategy as easy as possible!

Managing Partner 101: A Guide to Successful Law Firm Leadership, Second Edition

By Lawrence G. Green

This ABA bestseller is designed to help managing partners, lawyers, and other legal professionals understand the role and responsibilities of a law firm's managing partner. The book will shorten the learning curve for mastering successful management techniques for the new or experienced managing partner, through helpful guidelines, tips, and examples presented throughout the text. Of particular value is the author's extensive experience and discussion on the importance of leadership to the effective managing partner.

Paralegals, Profitability & the Future of Your Law Practice

By Arthur G. Greene and Therese A. Cannon

The book is your essential guide to effectively integrating paralegals into your practice. Learn the ethical issues involved in working with paralegals as well as how to handle conflicts of interest, supervision, timekeeping, compensation, billing, and much more. In addition, numerous forms and guidelines such as performance appraisals and a job description booklet are featured in the appendix as well as on the accompanying CD-ROM!

Results-Oriented Financial Management: A Step-By-Step Guide to Law Firm Profitability, Second Edition

By John G. Iezzi, CPA

This hands-on, how-to book will assist managing partners, law firm managers, and law firm accountants by providing them with the budgeting and financial knowledge they need to need to make the critical decisions. Whether you're a financial novice or veteran manager, this book will help you examine every facet of your financial affairs from cash flow and budget creation to billing and compensation. Also included with the book are valuable financial models on CD-ROM allowing you to compute profitability and determine budgets by inputting your own data. The appendix contains useful forms and examples from lawyers who have actually implemented alternative billing methods at their firms

Winning Alternatives to the Billable Hour: Strategies that Work, Second Edition

Edited by James A. Calloway and Mark A. Robertson

Find out how to initiate and implement different billing methods that make sense for you and your client. You'll learn how to explain—clearly and persuasively—the economic and client service advantages in changing billing methods. You'll discover how to establish a win-win billing situation with your clients no matter which method you choose. Written for lawyers in firms of all sizes, this book provides valuable examples, practical tools, and tips throughout. The appendix contains useful forms and examples from lawyers who have actually implemented alternative billing methods at their firms.

30-Day Risk-Free Order Form
Call Today! 1-800-285-2221
Monday–Friday, 7:30 AM – 5:30 PM, Central Time

Qty	Title	LPM Price	Regular Price	Total
_____	Compensation Plans for Law Firms, Fourth Edition (5110507)	79.95	94.95	$_____
_____	The Essential Formbook: Volume I (5110424V1)	169.95	199.95	$_____
_____	The Essential Formbook: Volume II (5110424V2)	169.95	199.95	$_____
_____	The Essential Formbook: Volume III (5110424V3)	169.95	199.95	$_____
_____	Law Office Procedures Manual, 2004 Fourth Edition (5110441)	109.95	129.95	$_____
_____	The Lawyer's Guide to Extranets (5110494)	59.95	69.95	$_____
_____	The Lawyer's Guide to Fact Finding on the Internet, Second Edition (5110497)	69.95	79.95	$_____
_____	The Lawyer's Guide to Fact Finding on the Internet, Combination Book and E-mail Newsletter (12 Issues) (511-0499P)	90.95	105.95	$_____
_____	The Lawyer's Guide to Marketing Your Practice, Second Edition (5110500)	79.95	89.95	$_____
_____	Managing Partner 101, Second Edition (5110451)	44.95	49.95	$_____
_____	Paralegals, Profitability & the Future of Your Law Practice (5110491)	59.95	69.95	$_____
_____	Results-Oriented Financial Management, Second Edition (5110493)	89.95	99.95	$_____
_____	Winning Alternatives to the Billable Hour, Second Edition (5110483)	$129.95	$149.95	$_____

*Postage and Handling	
$10.00 to $24.99	$5.95
$25.00 to $49.99	$9.95
$50.00 to $99.99	$12.95
$100.00 to $349.99	$17.95
$350 to $499.99	$24.95

**Tax
DC residents add 5.75%
IL residents add 8.75%
MD residents add 5%

Subtotal	$_____
*Postage and Handling	$_____
**Tax	$_____
TOTAL	$_____

PAYMENT

❑ Check enclosed (to the ABA)
❑ Visa   ❑ MasterCard   ❑ American Express

_____
Account Number   Exp. Date   Signature

Name _____ Firm _____
Address _____
City _____ State _____ Zip _____
Phone Number _____ E-Mail Address _____

Note: E-Mail address is required if ordering the
The Lawyer's Guide to Fact Finding on the Internet
E-mail Newsletter (5110498)

Guarantee
If—for any reason—you are not satisfied with your purchase, you may
return it within 30 days of receipt for a complete refund of the price of the
book(s). No questions asked!

Mail: ABA Publication Orders, P.O. Box 10892, Chicago, Illinois 60610-0892
♦ Phone: 1-800-285-2221 ♦ FAX: 312-988-5568

E-Mail: abasvcctr@abanet.org ♦ Internet: http://www.lawpractice.org/catalog

CUSTOMER COMMENT FORM

Title of Book: _____

We've tried to make this publication as useful, accurate, and readable as possible. Please take 5 minutes to tell us if we succeeded. Your comments and suggestions will help us improve our publications. Thank you!

1. How did you acquire this publication:

☐ by mail order   ☐ at a meeting/convention   ☐ as a gift

☐ by phone order   ☐ at a bookstore   ☐ don't know

☐ other: (describe) _____

Please rate this publication as follows:

	Excellent	Good	Fair	Poor	Not Applicable
Readability: Was the book easy to read and understand?	☐	☐	☐	☐	☐
Examples/Cases: Were they helpful, practical? Were there enough?	☐	☐	☐	☐	☐
Content: Did the book meet your expectations? Did it cover the subject adequately?	☐	☐	☐	☐	☐
Organization and clarity: Was the sequence of text logical? Was it easy to find what you wanted to know?	☐	☐	☐	☐	☐
Illustrations/forms/checklists: Were they clear and useful? Were there enough?	☐	☐	☐	☐	☐
Physical attractiveness: What did you think of the appearance of the publication (typesetting, printing, etc.)?	☐	☐	☐	☐	☐

Would you recommend this book to another attorney/administrator? ☐ Yes ☐ No

How could this publication be improved? What else would you like to see in it?

_____

_____

_____

Do you have other comments or suggestions? _____

_____

Name _____

Firm/Company _____

Address _____

City/State/Zip _____

Phone _____

Firm Size: _____ Area of specialization: _____

We appreciate your time and help.

Fold

BUSINESS REPLY MAIL

FIRST CLASS   PERMIT NO. 16471   CHICAGO, ILLINOIS

POSTAGE WILL BE PAID BY ADDRESSEE

AMERICAN BAR ASSOCIATION
PPM, 8th FLOOR
750 N. LAKE SHORE DRIVE
CHICAGO, ILLINOIS 60611-9851

Fold

LAW PRACTICE MANAGEMENT SECTION

MARKETING • MANAGEMENT • TECHNOLOGY • FINANCE

JOIN the ABA Law Practice Management Section (LPM) and receive significant discounts on future LPM book purchases! You'll also get direct access to marketing, management, technology, and finance tools that help lawyers and other professionals meet the demands of today's challenging legal environment.

Exclusive Membership Benefits Include:

- **Law Practice Magazine**
  Eight annual issues of our award-winning *Law Practice* magazine, full of insightful articles and practical tips on Marketing/Client Development, Practice Management, Legal Technology, and Finance.
- **ABA TECHSHOW®**
  Receive a $100 discount on ABA TECHSHOW, the world's largest legal technology conference!
- **LPM Book Discount**
  LPM has over eighty titles in print! Books topics cover the four core areas of law practice management – marketing, management, technology, and finance – as well as legal career issues.
- **Law Practice Today**
  LPM's unique web-based magazine in which the features change weekly! Law Practice Today covers all the hot topics in law practice management *today* – current issues, current challenges, current solutions.
- **Discounted CLE & Other Educational Opportunities**
  The Law Practice Management Section sponsors more than 100 educational sessions annually. LPM also offers other live programs, teleconferences and web cast seminars.
- **LawPractice.news**
  This monthly eUpdate brings information on Section news and activities, educational opportunities, and details on book releases and special offers.

Complete the membership application below.

Applicable Dues:
o$40 for ABA members   o$5 for ABA Law Student Division members

(ABA Membership is a prerequisite to membership in the Section. To join the ABA, call the Service Center at 1-800-285-2221.)

Method of Payment:
oBill me   Charge to my: oVisa   oMasterCard   oAmerican Express
Card number _____   Exp. Date _____
Signature _____   Date _____

Applicant's Information (please print):
Name _____   ABA I.D. number _____
Firm/Organization _____
Address _____   City/State/Zip _____
Telephone _____   FAX _____   Email _____

Fax your application to 312-988-5528 or join by phone: 1-800-285-2221, TDD 312-988-5168
Join online at www.lawpractice.org.

About the CD

The accompanying CD contains twenty-eight files that correspond to the twenty-five exhibits as listed on pages ix-x in the table of contents for *Anatomy of a Law Firm Merger, Third Edition*. The files with the extension "doc" (such as "Exhibit01.doc") contain the exhibits in Microsoft® Word for Windows format. Exhibits 17, 18, and 19 are also included in Microsoft® Excel format (named "exhibit017.xls", "exhibit018.xls", and "exhibit019.xls", respectively) for your convenience.

The file formats allow you to easily read and customize the material to your needs.

For additional information about the files on the CD, please open and read the "**readme.doc**" file on the CD.

NOTE: The set of files on the CD may only be used on a single computer or moved to and used on another computer. Under no circumstances may the set of files be used on more than one computer at one time. If you are interested in obtaining a license to use the set of files on a local network, please contact: Director, Copyrights and Contracts, American Bar Association, 321 North Clark Street, Chicago, IL 60610, (312) 988-6101. **Please read the license and warranty statements on the following page before using this CD.**

**Defending Liberty
Pursuing Justice**

CD-ROM to accompany
Anatomy of a Law Firm Merger, Third Edition